THE YALE SHAKESPEARE

Revised Edition

General Editors

Helge Kökeritz and Charles T. Prouty

THE TRAGEDY OF
JULIUS CAESAR

Edited by Alvin Kernan

NEW HAVEN AND LONDON
YALE UNIVERSITY PRESS

Library of Congress catalog card number: 59–8416

Revised Edition, April 1959
Fifth Printing, 1969

Preface of the General Editors

AS the late Professor Tucker Brooke has observed, practically all modern editions of Shakespeare are 18th-century versions of the plays, based on the additions, alterations, and emendations of editors of that period. It has been our purpose, as it was Professor Brooke's, to give the modern reader Shakespeare's plays in the approximate form of their original appearance.

About half the plays appeared in quarto form before the publication of the First Folio in 1623. Thus for a large number of plays the only available text is that of the Folio. In the case of quarto plays our policy has been to use that text as the basis of the edition, unless it is clear that the text has been contaminated.

Interesting for us today is the fact that there are no act or scene divisions in the Quartos with the exception of *Othello*, which does mark Acts I, II, IV, and V but lacks indications of scenes. Even in the Folio, although act divisions are generally noted, only a part of the scenes are divided. In no case, either in Quarto or Folio, is there any indication of the place of action. The manifold scene divisions for the battle in such a play as *Antony and Cleopatra*, together with such locations as "Another part of the field," are the additions of the 18th century.

We have eliminated all indications of the place and time of action, because there is no authority for them in the originals and because Shakespeare gives such information, when it is requisite for understanding the play, through the dialogue of the actors. We have been sparing in our use of added scene and, in some cases, act divisions, because these frequently impede the flow of the action, which in Shakespeare's time was curiously like that of modern films.

Spelling has been modernized except when the original clearly indicates a pronunciation unlike our own, e.g. *desart* (desert), *divel* (devil), *banket* (banquet), and often in such Elizabethan syncopations as *stolne* (stol'n), and *tane* (ta'en). In reproducing such forms we have followed the inconsistent usage of the original.

We have also preserved the original capitalization when this is a part of the meaning. In like manner we have tended to adopt the lineation of the original in many cases where modern editors print prose as verse or verse as prose. We have, moreover, followed the original punctuation wherever it was practicable.

In verse we print a final *-ed* to indicate its full syllabic value, otherwise *'d*. In prose we have followed the inconsistencies of the original in this respect.

Our general practice has been to include in footnotes all information a reader needs for immediate understanding of the given page. In somewhat empiric fashion we repeat glosses as we think the reader needs to be reminded of the meaning. Further information is given in notes (indicated by the letter *N* in the footnotes) to be found at the back of each volume. Appendices deal with the text and sources of the play.

Square brackets indicate material not found in the original text. Long emendations or lines taken from another authoritative text of a play are indicated in the footnotes for the information of the reader. We have silently corrected obvious typographical errors.

CONTENTS

[THE ACTORS' NAMES

JULIUS CAESAR

OCTAVIUS CAESAR
MARC ANTONY } *triumvirs after the death*
LEPIDUS *of Julius Caesar*

CICERO
PUBLIUS } *senators*
POPILIUS LENA

MARCUS BRUTUS
CAIUS CASSIUS
CASCA
TREBONIUS *conspirators against*
LIGARIUS *Julius Caesar*
DECIUS BRUTUS
METELLUS CIMBER
CINNA

FLAVIUS *and* MARULLUS, *tribunes*
ARTEMIDORUS, *a Sophist of Cnidos*
SOOTHSAYER
CINNA, *a poet*
POET, *Marcus Phaonius*

LUCILIUS
TITINIUS
MESSALA } *friends of Brutus and Cassius*
YOUNG CATO
VOLUMNIUS

VARRUS   STRATO
CLITUS   LUCIUS } *servants of Brutus*
CLAUDIO   DARDANIUS
PINDARUS, *servant of Cassius*

CALPURNIA, *wife to Caesar*
PORTIA, *wife to Brutus*

Commoners, or plebeians, of Rome; senators, guards, attendants]

THE TRAGEDY OF JULIUS CAESAR

Act I

SCENE 1

Enter Flavius, Marullus, and certain commoners
over the stage.

Flavius. Hence! home you idle creatures, get you
home.
Is this a holiday? What, know you not,
Being mechanical, you ought not walk
Upon a laboring day without the sign
Of your profession? Speak, what trade art thou? 5
Carpenter. Why, sir, a carpenter.
Marullus. Where is thy leather apron, and thy rule?
What dost thou with thy best apparel on?
You, sir, what trade are you? 9
Cobbler. Truly, sir, in respect of a fine workman,
I am but as you would say, a cobbler.
Marullus. But what trade art thou? Answer me
directly.
Cobbler. A trade, sir, that I hope I may use with a

SD **Marullus** N. (SD is used throughout to indicate stage direction; N refers to the corresponding note given at the end of the
text.) 3 **mechanical** members of the working class. 4–5 **sign . . .
profession** workers' clothing and tools. 10 **in respect of** compared
to. 11 **cobbler** pun on two meanings of word, 'shoe-repairer' and
'bungler.' 12 **directly** straightforwardly.

1

safe conscience, which is indeed, sir, a mender of bad
soles.   15

Flavius. What trade thou knave? thou naughty
knave, what trade?

Cobbler. Nay, I beseech you, sir, be not out with me:
yet, if you be out, sir, I can mend you.

Marullus. What mean'st thou by that? Mend me,
thou saucy fellow?   20

Cobbler. Why, sir, cobble you.

Flavius. Thou art a cobbler, art thou?

Cobbler. Truly, sir, all that I live by is with the
awl: I meddle with no tradesman's matters, nor
women's matters, but withal I am indeed, sir, a sur-
geon to old shoes, when they are in great danger, I
recover them. As proper men as ever trod upon neat's
leather have gone upon my handiwork.   28

Flavius. But wherefore art not in thy shop today?
Why dost thou lead these men about the streets?

Cobbler. Truly, sir, to wear out their shoes, to get
myself into more work. But, indeed, sir, we make
holiday to see Caesar and to rejoice in his triumph.

Marullus. Wherefore rejoice? What conquest
brings he home?

What tributaries follow him to Rome   35
To grace in captive bonds his chariot wheels?
You blocks, you stones, you worse than senseless
things!
O you hard hearts, you cruel men of Rome,
Knew you not Pompey? Many a time and oft
Have you climb'd up to walls and battlements,   40

15 **soles** a pun on shoe soles and souls. 16 **Flavius** N. **naughty**
worthless. 18 **out** angry, out of temper. 19 **out . . . mend** N.
27 **proper** true, fine. 28–9 **neat's leather** cowhide. 33 **triumph** N.
35 **tributaries** prisoners, payers of tribute.

2

To towers and windows, yea, to chimney tops,
Your infants in your arms, and there have sat
The livelong day, with patient expectation,
To see great Pompey pass the streets of Rome.
And when you saw his chariot but appear,   45
Have you not made a universal shout,
That Tiber trembled underneath her banks
To hear the replication of your sounds
Made in her concave shores?
And do you now put on your best attire?   50
And do you now cull out a holiday?
And do you now strew flowers in his way,
That comes in triumph over Pompey's blood?
Be gone!
Run to your houses, fall upon your knees,   55
Pray to the gods to intermit the plague
That needs must light on this ingratitude.
    Flavius. Go, go, good countrymen, and for this
        fault
Assemble all the poor men of your sort;
Draw them to Tiber banks, and weep your tears   60
Into the channel, till the lowest stream
Do kiss the most exalted shores of all.
                              Exeunt all the commoners.
See where their basest mettle be not mov'd,
They vanish tongue-tied in their guiltiness.
Go you down that way towards the Capitol,   65
This way will I. Disrobe the images
If you do find them deck'd with ceremonies.
    Marullus. May we do so?
You know it is the feast of Lupercal.

48 **replication** repetition. 51 **cull out** pick this as. 56 **intermit**
prevent. 62 **exalted** highest. 63 **where** shorter form of 'whether.'
mettle quality of temperament. 66–7 **images . . . ceremonies** N.
69 **Lupercal** N.

3

Flavius. It is no matter, let no images   70
Be hung with Caesar's trophies. I'll about
And drive away the vulgar from the streets.
So do you too where you perceive them thick.
These growing feathers pluck'd from Caesar's wing
Will make him fly an ordinary pitch,   75
Who else would soar above the view of men
And keep us all in servile fearfulness.   *Exeunt.*

SCENE 2

*Enter Caesar, Antony for the course, Calpurnia,
Portia, Decius, Cicero, Brutus, Cassius, Casca, a
  Soothsayer: after them Marullus and Flavius.*

Caesar. Calpurnia!
Casca.   Peace, ho! Caesar speaks.
Caesar.   Calpurnia!
Calpurnia. Here my lord.
Caesar. Stand you directly in Antonio's way
When he doth run his course. Antonio!
Antony. Caesar, my lord.   5
Caesar. Forget not in your speed, Antonio,
To touch Calpurnia, for our elders say,
The barren touched in this holy chase
Shake off their sterile curse.
Antony.   I shall remember.
When Caesar says, 'Do this,' it is perform'd.   10

72 **vulgar** commoners. 75 **pitch** high point of a falcon's flight
before diving on its prey. 76 **above . . . men** out of human sight.
Scene 2 N. SD **Antony . . . Calpurnia** N. **for the course** prepared for the race. 1 **Calpurnia . . . Calpurnia** N.
  4

Caesar. Set on, and leave no ceremony out.

Soothsayer. Caesar.

Caesar. Ha! Who calls?

Casca. Bid every noise be still, peace yet again.

Caesar. Who is it in the press that calls on me?   15
I hear a tongue shriller than all the music
Cry 'Caesar.' Speak, Caesar is turn'd to hear.

Soothsayer. Beware the ides of March.

Caesar. What man is that?

Brutus. A soothsayer bids you beware the ides of
    March.   20

Caesar. Set him before me, let me see his face.

Cassius. Fellow, come from the throng, look upon
    Caesar.

Caesar. What say'st thou to me now? Speak once
    again.

Soothsayer. Beware the ides of March.

Caesar. He is a dreamer, let us leave him. Pass.   25
    Sennet. Exeunt. Manent Brutus and Cassius.

Cassius. Will you go see the order of the course?

Brutus. Not I.

Cassius. I pray you, do.

Brutus. I am not gamesome. I do lack some part
Of that quick spirit that is in Antony.   30
Let me not hinder, Cassius, your desires;
I'll leave you.

Cassius. Brutus, I do observe you now of late.
I have not from your eyes that gentleness
And show of love as I was wont to have;   35

11 **Set on** proceed. 15 **press** crowd. 18 **ides of March** March 15·
SD **Sennet** set of notes on trumpet signaling a ceremonial
entrance or exit. 26 **order of the course** progress of the race.
29 **gamesome** fond of games. 35 **show** manifestation. **wont** accustomed.

You bear too stubborn and too strange a hand
Over your friend that loves you.
  Brutus.   Cassius,
Be not deceiv'd; if I have veil'd my look,
I turn the trouble of my countenance
Merely upon myself. Vexed I am   40
Of late with passions of some difference,
Conceptions only proper to myself,
Which give some soil, perhaps, to my behaviors,
But let not therefore my good friends be griev'd—
Among which number, Cassius, be you one—   45
Nor construe any further my neglect,
Than that poor Brutus, with himself at war,
Forgets the shows of love to other men.
  Cassius. Then, Brutus, I have much mistook your
      passion,   49
By means whereof this breast of mine hath buried
Thoughts of great value, worthy cogitations.
Tell me, good Brutus, can you see your face?
  Brutus. No, Cassius, for the eye sees not itself
But by reflection by some other things.
  Cassius. 'Tis just,   55
And it is very much lamented, Brutus,
That you have no such mirrors as will turn
Your hidden worthiness into your eye,

36–7 bear . . . friend treat your friend too stiffly; the figure
here is of managing a horse with Brutus as the horseman and
Cassius as the horse. 39–40 turn . . . myself my troubled countenance results entirely from my own problems. 40 **Merely** entirely.
41 **of some difference** conflicting. 42 **proper** pertaining. 43 **soil**
taint. 46 **construe . . . further** make more of. **construe** stressed
– —. 50 **By means whereof** because of which. 51 **worthy** important. 55 **just** exactly so. 57 **turn** reflect.

That you might see your shadow. I have heard
Where many of the best respect in Rome—   60
Except immortal Caesar—speaking of Brutus,
And groaning underneath this age's yoke,
Have wish'd that noble Brutus had his eyes.
  Brutus. Into what dangers would you lead me,
      Cassius,
That you would have me seek into myself   65
For that which is not in me?
  Cassius. Therefore, good Brutus, be prepar'd to
      hear,
And, since you know you cannot see yourself
So well as by reflection, I, your glass,
Will modestly discover to yourself   70
That of yourself which you yet know not of.
And be not jealous on me, gentle Brutus:
Were I a common laughter, or did use
To stale with ordinary oaths my love
To every new protester; if you know   75
That I do fawn on men, and hug them hard,
And after scandal them; or if you know
That I profess myself in banqueting
To all the rout, then hold me dangerous.
                              Flourish and shout.
  Brutus. What means this shouting?   80
I do fear the people choose Caesar for their king.

59 shadow image. 60 respect quality. 63 had his eyes were aware
of his own merit. 69 glass mirror. 70 modestly discover disclose
in a manner which will spare your modesty, i.e. without exaggera-
tion. 72 jealous suspicious. 73 laughter joke, object of humor.
use were accustomed to. 74 stale make common. 75 protester one
who solemnly avers his love. 77 scandal defame. 78 profess open
up, reveal. 79 rout crowd. SD Flourish sounding of trumpets.

Cassius. Ay, do you fear it?
Then must I think you would not have it so.
  Brutus. I would not, Cassius, yet I love him well.
But wherefore do you hold me here so long?   85
What is it that you would impart to me?
If it be aught toward the general good,
Set honor in one eye and death i' th' other,
And I will look on both indifferently;
For let the gods so speed me as I love   90
The name of honor more than I fear death.
  Cassius. I know that virtue to be in you, Brutus,
As well as I do know your outward favor.
Well, honor is the subject of my story.
I cannot tell what you and other men   95
Think of this life, but for my single self
I had as lief not be as live to be
In awe of such a thing as I myself.
I was born free as Caesar, so were you.
We both have fed as well, and we can both   100
Endure the winter's cold as well as he.
For once, upon a raw and gusty day,
The troubled Tiber chafing with her shores,
Caesar said to me, 'Dar'st thou, Cassius, now
Leap in with me into this angry flood,   105
And swim to yonder point?' Upon the word,
Accoutred as I was, I plunged in
And bade him follow; so indeed he did.
The torrent roar'd, and we did buffet it
With lusty sinews, throwing it aside   110

87 **general good** public welfare. 89 **indifferently** impartially, and without fear. 90 **speed** advance. 93 **favor** features. 97 **lief . . . live** pun based on Elizabethan pronunciation of both words as 'lieve.' 98 **thing . . . myself** a man as I am. 103 **chafing with** raging against. 107 **Accoutred** dressed.

8

And stemming it with hearts of controversy.
But ere we could arrive the point propos'd,
Caesar cried, 'Help me, Cassius, or I sink!'
I, as Aeneas, our great ancestor,
Did from the flames of Troy upon his shoulder   115
The old Anchises bear, so from the waves of Tiber
Did I the tired Caesar. And this man
Is now become a god, and Cassius is
A wretched creature and must bend his body
If Caesar carelessly but nod on him.   120
He had a fever when he was in Spain,
And when the fit was on him I did mark
How he did shake. 'Tis true, this god did shake.
His coward lips did from their color fly,   124
And that same eye whose bend doth awe the world
Did lose his luster. I did hear him groan.
Ay, and that tongue of his that bade the Romans
Mark him and write his speeches in their books,
'Alas,' it cried, 'Give me some drink, Titinius,'
As a sick girl. Ye gods, it does amaze me   130
A man of such a feeble temper should
So get the start of the majestic world
And bear the palm alone.   *Shout. Flourish.*
  Brutus.   Another general shout?
I do believe that these applauses are   134
For some new honors that are heap'd on Caesar.

111 stemming making headway against. hearts of controversy
hearts filled with rivalry. 113 Caesar . . . sink N. 114 Aeneas,
our great ancestor N. 119 bend his body bow. 124 from their
color fly the lips turned pale like cowardly soldiers abandoning
their flag. 125 bend glance. 126 his regular Elizabethan form of
neuter possessive pronoun 'its.' 128 books writing tablets. 130
amaze mystify. 131 temper spirit. 132 get the start outstrip in a
race. 133 bear the palm win the prize.

Cassius. Why, man, he doth bestride the narrow
    world
Like a Colossus, and we petty men
Walk under his huge legs and peep about
To find ourselves dishonorable graves.
Men at some time are masters of their fates.   140
The fault, dear Brutus, is not in our stars,
But in ourselves, that we are underlings.
Brutus and Caesar: what should be in that 'Caesar'?
Why should that name be sounded more than yours?
Write them together, yours is as fair a name;   145
Sound them, it doth become the mouth as well;
Weigh them, it is as heavy; conjure with 'em,
'Brutus' will start a spirit as soon as 'Caesar.'
Now in the names of all the gods at once,
Upon what meat doth this our Caesar feed   150
That he is grown so great? Age, thou art sham'd.
Rome, thou hast lost the breed of noble bloods.
When went there by an age, since the great flood,
But it was fam'd with more than with one man?   154
When could they say, till now, that talk'd of Rome,
That her wide walks encompass'd but one man?
Now is it Rome indeed and room enough
When there is in it but one only man.
O! you and I have heard our fathers say,   159
There was a Brutus once that would have brook'd

137 **Colossus** a gigantic bronze statue of Apollo supposed to have
stood across the harbor at Rhodes. 141 **stars** referring to the
belief that the position of the stars determines the fates of men.
148 **start a spirit** raise up a ghost. 152 **bloods** men of courage and
fire. 154 **fam'd with** made famous by. 156 **encompass'd** enclosed.
157 **Rome . . . room** a pun based on the Elizabethan pronunciation of *Rome* as *room*. 160 **Brutus** Lucius Junius, the ancestor of
Marcus Brutus, who expelled the Tarquin kings. **brook'd** tolerated.

Th' eternal divell to keep his state in Rome
As easily as a king.

Brutus. That you do love me, I am nothing jealous;
What you would work me to, I have some aim;
How I have thought of this and of these times,   165
I shall recount hereafter. For this present,
I would not so, with love I might entreat you,
Be any further mov'd. What you have said
I will consider; what you have to say
I will with patience hear, and find a time   170
Both meet to hear and answer such high things.
Till then, my noble friend, chew upon this:
Brutus had rather be a villager
Than to repute himself a son of Rome
Under these hard conditions, as this time   175
Is like to lay upon us.

Cassius.   I am glad
That my weak words have struck but thus much show
Of fire from Brutus.

Enter Caesar and his train.

Brutus. The games are done and Caesar is return-
          ing.   179
Cassius. As they pass by, pluck Casca by the sleeve,
And he will, after his sour fashion, tell you
What hath proceeded worthy note today.
Brutus. I will do so, but look you, Cassius,
The angry spot doth glow on Caesar's brow,
And all the rest look like a chidden train: 185

161 **divell** devil, the spelling indicates the old pronunciation.
keep . . . state maintain his court. 163 **nothing** not at all.
jealous suspicious. 164 **work** shape. **aim** understanding. 166 **For**
. . . present for the moment. 168 **mov'd** urged. 171 **meet** fit.
175 **as** such as. 182 **proceeded . . . note** happened of interest.

11

Calpurnia's cheek is pale, and Cicero
Looks with such ferret and such fiery eyes
As we have seen him in the Capitol,
Being cross'd in conference by some senators.
  Cassius. Casca will tell us what the matter is.   190
  Caesar. Antonio!
  Antony. Caesar.
  Caesar. Let me have men about me that are fat,
Sleek-headed men, and such as sleep a-nights.
Yond Cassius has a lean and hungry look,   195
He thinks too much, such men are dangerous.
  Antony. Fear him not, Caesar, he's not dangerous.
He is a noble Roman and well given.
  Caesar. Would he were fatter, but I fear him not.
Yet if my name were liable to fear,   200
I do not know the man I should avoid
So soon as that spare Cassius. He reads much,
He is a great observer, and he looks
Quite through the deeds of men. He loves no plays,
As thou dost, Antony; he hears no music;   205
Seldom he smiles, and smiles in such a sort
As if he mock'd himself and scorn'd his spirit
That could be mov'd to smile at anything.
Such men as he be never at heart's ease
Whiles they behold a greater than themselves,   210
And therefore are they very dangerous.
I rather tell thee what is to be fear'd
Than what I fear, for always I am Caesar.
Come on my right hand, for this ear is deaf,

187 **ferret** red like a ferret's. 189 **cross'd in conference** opposed in debate. 198 **well given** well disposed. 203–4 **looks . . . deeds** sees through outward appearances to the motives. 204–5 **He . . . music** N. 206 **sort** way. 209 **be** are; *be* is commonly used as plural by Shakespeare. 214 **deaf** N.

12

And tell me truly, what thou think'st of him. 215
    Sennet. Exeunt Caesar and his train.
  Casca. You pull'd me by the cloak, would you speak
with me?
  Brutus. Ay, Casca; tell us what hath chanc'd today
That Caesar looks so sad.
  Casca. Why, you were with him, were you not? 220
  Brutus. I should not then ask Casca what had
    chanc'd.
  Casca. Why, there was a crown offer'd him, and
being offer'd him, he put it by with the back of his
hand, thus, and then the people fell a-shouting.
  Brutus. What was the second noise for? 225
  Casca. Why, for that too.
  Cassius. They shouted thrice, what was the last cry
for?
  Casca. Why, for that too.
  Brutus. Was the crown offer'd him thrice? 230
  Casca. Ay, marry was't, and he put it by thrice,
every time gentler than other; and at every putting-
by mine honest neighbors shouted.
  Cassius. Who offer'd him the crown?
  Casca. Why, Antony. 235
  Brutus. Tell us the manner of it, gentle Casca.
  Casca. I can as well be hang'd as tell the manner of
it. It was mere foolery, I did not mark it. I saw Mark
Antony offer him a crown—yet 'twas not a crown
neither, 'twas one of these coronets—and, as I told
you, he put it by once, but, for all that, to my thinking, he would fain have had it. Then he offered it to
him again, then he put it by again, but to my think-

218 chanc'd happened. 219 sad serious. 223 put it by pushed it
aside. 233 neighbors those in the crowd around. 238 mere entirely. mark pay close attention to. 240 coronets laurel garlands.

ing, he was very loath to lay his fingers off it. And then he offered it the third time, he put it the third time by, and still as he refus'd it the rabblement hooted, and clapp'd their chopt hands, and threw up their sweaty nightcaps, and uttered such a deal of stinking breath because Caesar refus'd the crown, that it had almost choked Caesar, for he swoonded and fell down at it. And for mine own part, I durst not laugh for fear of opening my lips and receiving the bad air.

Cassius. But soft, I pray you; what, did Caesar swound? 254

Casca. He fell down in the marketplace, and foam'd at mouth, and was speechless.

Brutus. 'Tis very like he hath the falling-sickness.

Cassius. No, Caesar hath it not; but you, and I, And honest Casca, we have the falling-sickness. 259

Casca. I know not what you mean by that, but I am sure Caesar fell down. If the tag-rag people did not clap him and hiss him, according as he pleas'd and displeas'd them, as they use to do the players in the theater, I am no true man. 264

Brutus. What said he, when he came unto himself?

Casca. Marry, before he fell down, when he perceiv'd the common herd was glad he refus'd the crown, he pluck'd me ope his doublet and offer'd them his throat to cut. And I had been a man of any occupation, if I would not have taken him at a word, I would I might go to hell among the rogues. And so he fell. When he came to himself again, he said if he had

246 still always. 247 chopt chapped, work-hardened. 248 deal large amount. 250 swoonded fainted. 254 soft wait. 257 very like probable. falling-sickness epilepsy. 261 tag-rag rabble. 263 use to do customarily do. 268 pluck'd me ope opened. doublet jacket. 269 And if. occupation trade.

14

done or said anything amiss, he desir'd their worships to think it was his infirmity. Three or four wenches, where I stood, cried, 'Alas, good soul,' and forgave him with all their hearts. But there's no heed to be taken of them; if Caesar had stabb'd their mothers, they would have done no less.

Brutus. And after that he came thus sad, away?

Casca. Ay.   280

Cassius. Did Cicero say anything?

Casca. Ay, he spoke Greek.

Cassius. To what effect?

Casca. Nay, and I tell you that, I'll ne'er look you i' th' face again. But those that understood him smil'd at one another and shook their heads; but for mine own part, it was Greek to me. I could tell you more news too: Marullus and Flavius, for pulling scarfs off Caesar's images, are put to silence. Fare you well. There was more foolery yet, if I could remember it.   291

Cassius. Will you sup with me tonight, Casca?

Casca. No, I am promis'd forth.

Cassius. Will you dine with me tomorrow?   294

Casca. Ay, if I be alive, and your mind hold, and your dinner worth the eating.

Cassius. Good, I will expect you.

Casca. Do so. Farewell, both.   *Exit.*

Brutus. What a blunt fellow is this grown to be. He was quick mettle when he went to school.   300

Cassius. So is he now in execution
Of any bold or noble enterprise,

273 **their worships** address of respect. 289 **put to silence** silenced. 293 **promis'd forth** promised to dine elsewhere. 300 **quick mettle** lively.

However he puts on this tardy form.
This rudeness is a sauce to his good wit,
Which gives men stomach to disgest his words   305
With better appetite.
    Brutus. And so it is. For this time I will leave you.
Tomorrow, if you please to speak with me,
I will come home to you; or, if you will
Come home to me, and I will wait for you.   310
    Cassius. I will do so. Till then, think of the world.
                                  Exit Brutus.
Well, Brutus, thou art noble; yet I see
Thy honorable mettle may be wrought
From that it is dispos'd; therefore it is meet
That noble minds keep ever with their likes,   315
For who so firm, that cannot be seduc'd?
Caesar doth bear me hard, but he loves Brutus.
If I were Brutus now and he were Cassius,
He should not humor me. I will this night,
In several hands, in at his windows throw,   320
As if they came from several citizens,
Writings, all tending to the great opinion
That Rome holds of his name, wherein obscurely
Caesar's ambition shall be glanced at.
And after this, let Caesar seat him sure,   325
For we will shake him, or worse days endure.   *Exit.*

303 **However** notwithstanding that. **tardy form** show of slowness.
304 **rudeness** roughness. **wit** intelligence. 305 **stomach** appetite.
disgest digest. 314 **From . . . dispos'd** contrary to its natural
form or direction. **meet** proper. 317 **bear me hard** dislike me.
319 **humor** influence. 320 **several hands** different handwritings.
322 **tending to** bearing on. 324 **glanced at** referred to. 325 **seat
him sure** put himself securely in power.

SCENE 3

Thunder and lightning. Enter Casca and Cicero.

Cicero. Good even, Casca; brought you Caesar
  home?
Why are you breathless, and why stare you so?
  Casca. Are not you mov'd, when all the sway of
  earth
Shakes like a thing unfirm? O Cicero,
I have seen tempests, when the scolding winds   5
Have riv'd the knotty oaks, and I have seen
Th' ambitious ocean swell, and rage, and foam,
To be exalted with the threat'ning clouds;
But never till tonight, never till now,
Did I go through a tempest dropping fire.   10
Either there is a civil strife in heaven,
Or else the world, too saucy with the gods,
Incenses them to send destruction.   13
  Cicero. Why, saw you anything more wonderful?
  Casca. A common slave, you know him well by sight,
Held up his left hand, which did flame and burn
Like twenty torches join'd; and yet his hand,
Not sensible of fire, remain'd unscorch'd.
Besides—I ha' not since put up my sword—
Against the Capitol I met a lion,   20
Who glaz'd upon me, and went surly by,
Without annoying me. And there were drawn

1 **brought** escorted. 3 **sway of earth** earthly realm. 8 **exalted**
raised up. 12 **saucy** insolent. 13 **destruction** four syllables here.
18 **sensible of** feeling. 20 **Against** near. 21 **glaz'd** stared fixedly.
22 **annoying** harming. 22–3 **drawn . . . heap** crowded together.

Upon a heap a hundred ghastly women,
Transformed with their fear, who swore they saw
Men all in fire walk up and down the streets.　　　25
And yesterday the bird of night did sit,
Even at noonday, upon the market place,
Hooting and shrieking. When these prodigies
Do so conjointly meet, let not men say,
'These are their reasons, they are natural.'　　　30
For, I believe they are portentous things
Unto the climate that they point upon.

Cicero. Indeed, it is a strange-disposed time.
But men may construe things after their fashion,
Clean from the purpose of the things themselves.　　　35
Comes Caesar to the Capitol tomorrow?

Casca. He doth, for he did bid Antonio
Send word to you he would be there tomorrow.　　　38

Cicero. Good night, then, Casca: this disturbed sky
Is not to walk in.

Casca.　　　　　　Farewell, Cicero.　　　*Exit Cicero.*

Enter Cassius.

Cassius. Who's there?

Casca.　　　　　　　A Roman.

Cassius.　　　　　　　　　　Casca, by your voice.

Casca. Your ear is good. Cassius, what night is
　　this?

Cassius. A very pleasing night to honest men.

Casca. Who ever knew the heavens menace so?

26 **bird of night** the owl, a bird of ill omen. 29 **conjointly** together.
30 **These . . . natural** these are normal events with understand-
able causes. 32 **climate** region. 33 **strange-disposed** abnormal.
34–5 **construe . . . themselves** apply their own theories to events
and distort the true meaning. 35 **Clean from** directly opposite to.
39 **sky** air.

18

Cassius. Those that have known the earth so full of
    faults.   45
For my part, I have walk'd about the streets,
Submitting me unto the perilous night,
And, thus unbraced, Casca, as you see,
Have bar'd my bosom to the thunderstone;   49
And when the cross blue lightning seem'd to open
The breast of heaven, I did present myself
Even in the aim and very flash of it.
  Casca. But wherefore did you so much tempt the
    heavens?
It is the part of men to fear and tremble
When the most mighty gods by tokens send   55
Such dreadful heralds to astonish us.
  Cassius. You are dull, Casca, and those sparks of
    life
That should be in a Roman, you do want,
Or else you use not. You look pale, and gaze,
And put on fear, and cast yourself in wonder,   60
To see the strange impatience of the heavens.
But if you would consider the true cause
Why all these fires, why all these gliding ghosts,
Why birds and beasts, from quality and kind,
Why old men, fools, and children calculate,   65
Why all these things change from their ordinance,
Their natures, and preformed faculties,

47 **perilous** dissyllabic, i.e. 'parlous.' 48 **unbraced** with doublet
open. 49 **thunderstone** thunderbolt. 50 **cross** jagged. 52 **Even . . .
aim** as the very center of the target. **Even** pronounce 'e'en.'
56 **astonish** amaze. 57 **dull** slow witted. 58 **want** lack. 60 **put on**
encourage. **cast . . . wonder** throw yourself into bewilderment.
64 **from . . . kind** contrary to natural character. 65 **calculate**
prophesy. 66 **ordinance** proper and ordained practice. 67 **preformed faculties** innate qualities.

To monstrous quality, why, you shall find
That heaven hath infus'd them with these spirits
To make them instruments of fear and warning   70
Unto some monstrous state.
Now could I, Casca, name to thee a man
Most like this dreadful night,
That thunders, lightens, opens graves, and roars
As doth the lion in the Capitol,   75
A man no mightier than thyself, or me,
In personal action, yet prodigious grown,
And fearful as these strange eruptions are.
  Casca. 'Tis Caesar that you mean, is it not, Cassius?
  Cassius. Let it be who it is, for Romans now   80
Have thews and limbs like to their ancestors;
But woe the while, our fathers' minds are dead,
And we are govern'd with our mothers' spirits,
Our yoke and sufferance show us womanish.
  Casca. Indeed, they say the senators tomorrow   85
Mean to establish Caesar as a king,
And he shall wear his crown by sea and land,
In every place, save here in Italy.
  Cassius. I know where I will wear this dagger then,
Cassius from bondage will deliver Cassius.   90
Therein, ye gods, you make the weak most strong,
Therein, ye gods, you tyrants do defeat.
Nor stony tower, nor walls of beaten brass,
Nor airless dungeon, nor strong links of iron
Can be retentive to the strength of spirit;   95

71 **monstrous state** unnatural condition of human affairs. **77 prodigious** threatening. **78 fearful** causing fright, not 'frightened.' **eruptions** disorders in nature. 81 **thews** sinews. 82 **woe the while** woe on these times. 84 **yoke and sufferance** patient acceptance of slavery. 93 **Nor** . . . **nor** neither . . . nor.
    20

But life being weary of these worldly bars
Never lacks power to dismiss itself.
If I know this, know all the world besides,
That part of tyranny that I do bear
I can shake off at pleasure.   *Thunder still.*
    Casca.   So can I,   100
So every bondman in his own hand bears
The power to cancel his captivity.
    Cassius. And why should Caesar be a tyrant then?
Poor man, I know he would not be a wolf
But that he sees the Romans are but sheep;   105
He were no lion, were not Romans hinds.
Those that with haste will make a mighty fire,
Begin it with weak straws. What trash is Rome,
What rubbish, and what offal, when it serves
For the base matter to illuminate   110
So vile a thing as Caesar. But, O Grief,
Where hast thou led me? I, perhaps, speak this
Before a willing bondman; then I know
My answer must be made. But I am arm'd,
And dangers are to me indifferent.   115
    Casca. You speak to Casca, and to such a man
That is no fleering telltale. Hold, my hand.
Be factious for redress of all these griefs,
And I will set this foot of mine as far   119
As who goes furthest.
    Cassius.   There's a bargain made.
Now know you, Casca, I have mov'd already
Some certain of the noblest-minded Romans

106 **He were** he would be. **hinds** deer, also servants. 111 **vile**
worthless. 114 **My answer . . . made** I shall have to answer for
what I have said. 117 **fleering** grinning. **my hand** offers his hand
as pledge. 118 **Be factious** assemble a party or faction. **griefs**
grievances. 120 **who** whoever.

21

To undergo, with me, an enterprise
Of honorable, dangerous consequence;
And I do know by this, they stay for me   125
In Pompey's porch, for now, this fearful night,
There is no stir, or walking in the streets,
And the complexion of the element
In favor's like the work we have in hand,
Most bloody, fiery, and most terrible.   130

Enter Cinna.

 Casca. Stand close awhile, for here comes one in
  haste.
 Cassius. 'Tis Cinna, I do know him by his gait,
He is a friend. Cinna, where haste you so?
 Cinna. To find out you. Who's that? Mettellus
  Cimber?
 Cassius. No, it is Casca; one incorporate   135
To our attempts. Am I not stay'd for, Cinna?
 Cinna. I am glad on't. What a fearful night is this!
There's two or three of us have seen strange sights.
 Cassius. Am I not stay'd for? Tell me.
 Cinna.   Yes, you are.
O Cassius, if you could   140
But win the noble Brutus to our party—
 Cassius. Be you content. Good Cinna, take this
  paper,
And look you lay it in the praetor's chair,
Where Brutus may but find it, and throw this
In at his window, set this up with wax   145

---

123 **undergo** undertake. 125 **by this** by this time. **stay for** await.
126 **Pompey's porch** N. 128 **complexion of the element** condition
of the sky. 129 **favor** appearance. 131 **Stand close** draw back
out of sight. 135 **incorporate** joined. 143 **praetor's chair** N.

Upon old Brutus' statue; all this done,
Repair to Pompey's porch, where you shall find us.
Is Decius Brutus and Trebonius there?
  Cinna. All but Metellus Cimber, and he's gone
To seek you at your house. Well, I will hie,   150
And so bestow these papers as you bade me.
  Cassius. That done, repair to Pompey's theater.
                                                    Exit Cinna.
Come, Casca, you and I will yet, ere day,
See Brutus at his house; three parts of him
Is ours already, and the man entire   155
Upon the next encounter yields him ours.
  Casca. O, he sits high in all the people's hearts,
And that which would appear offense in us,
His countenance, like richest alchemy,
Will change to virtue and to worthiness.   160
  Cassius. Him, and his worth, and our great need of
    him,
You have right well conceited. Let us go,
For it is after midnight, and ere day
We will awake him and be sure of him.   *Exeunt.*

146 **old Brutus** Lucius Junius Brutus. 147 **Repair** return. 150 **hie** hasten. 156 **encounter** meeting. **yields him ours** joins our party. 159 **countenance** support, agreement. **alchemy** the science of turning base metals into gold. 160 **worthiness** nobleness. 162 **conceited** understood.

Act II

SCENE 1

Enter Brutus in his orchard.

Brutus. What, Lucius, ho!
I cannot, by the progress of the stars,
Give guess how near to day. Lucius, I say!
I would it were my fault to sleep so soundly.   4
When, Lucius, when? Awake, I say! What, Lucius!

Enter Lucius.

Lucius. Call'd you, my lord?
Brutus. Get me a taper in my study, Lucius.
When it is lighted, come and call me here.
Lucius. I will, my lord.   *Exit.*
Brutus. It must be by his death, and for my part
I know no personal cause to spurn at him,   11
But for the general. He would be crown'd.
How that might change his nature, there's the ques-
          tion.
It is the bright day that brings forth the adder,
And that craves wary walking. Crown him that,   15
And then I grant we put a sting in him
That at his will he may do danger with.
Th' abuse of greatness is when it disjoins

SD **orchard** garden. 5 **When** exclamation of impatience. **7 taper**
candle. 11 **spurn** to strike or kick. 12 **general** public good.
17 **danger** harm. 18 **disjoins** separates.

24

Remorse from power, and, to speak truth of Caesar,
I have not known when his affections sway'd   20
More than his reason. But 'tis a common proof
That lowliness is young ambition's ladder,
Whereto the climber upward turns his face;
But when he once attains the upmost round,
He then unto the ladder turns his back,   25
Looks in the clouds, scorning the base degrees
By which he did ascend. So Caesar may;
Then, lest he may, prevent. And, since the quarrel
Will bear no color for the thing he is,
Fashion it thus: that what he is, augmented,   30
Would run to these and these extremities,
And therefore think him as a serpent's egg
Which hatch'd, would, as his kind, grow mischievous,
And kill him in the shell.

Enter Lucius.

Lucius. The taper burneth in your closet, sir.   35
Searching the window for a flint, I found
This paper, thus seal'd up, and I am sure
It did not lie there when I went to bed.
                                        Gives him the letter.
Brutus. Get you to bed again, it is not day.
Is not tomorrow, boy, the first of March?   40
    Lucius. I know not, sir.

19 **Remorse** pity. 20 **affections** feelings. **sway'd** controlled him.
21 **common proof** general experience. 24 **round** rung. 26 **base
degrees** low steps literally, but also the common people whom
Caesar courted in his rise to power. 28 **prevent** forestall him.
quarrel cause of complaint. 29 **color** pretense N. 30 **Fashion**
construct the argument. 31 **these and these** such and such.
33 **as his kind** according to its nature. **mischievous** harmful.
35 **closet** study, private room. 40 **first of March** N.

Brutus. Look in the calendar and bring me word.
Lucius. I will, sir.   *Exit.*
Brutus. The exhalations whizzing in the air
Give so much light that I may read by them.   45
                    Opens the letter, and reads.
'Brutus, thou sleep'st; awake, and see thyself.
Shall Rome, &c. Speak, strike, redress!
Brutus, thou sleep'st; awake!'
Such instigations have been often dropp'd
Where I have took them up.   50
'Shall Rome, &c.' Thus must I piece it out:
Shall Rome stand under one man's awe? What,
    Rome?
My ancestors did from the streets of Rome
The Tarquin drive, when he was call'd a king.
'Speak, strike, redress!' Am I entreated   55
To speak, and strike? O Rome, I make thee promise,
If the redress will follow, thou receivest
Thy full petition at the hand of Brutus.

                    Enter Lucius.

Lucius. Sir, March is wasted fifteen days.   59
                    Knocking within.
Brutus. 'Tis good. Go to the gate, somebody knocks.
Since Cassius first did whet me against Caesar,
I have not slept.
Between the acting of a dreadful thing
And the first motion, all the interim is
Like a phantasma, or a hideous dream: 65
The genius and the mortal instruments

44 exhalations meteors. 52 under . . . awe in awe of one man.
59 fifteen N. 64 motion thought. 65 phantasma nightmare.
66 genius guardian spirit. mortal instruments the parts of the
body.
    26

Are then in council; and the state of a man,
Like to a little kingdom, suffers then
The nature of an insurrection.   69

Enter Lucius.

Lucius. Sir, 'tis your brother Cassius at the door,
Who doth desire to see you.
Brutus.   Is he alone?
Lucius. No, sir, there are moe with him.
Brutus.   Do you know them?
Lucius. No, sir; their hats are pluck'd about their
    ears,
And half their faces buried in their cloaks,
That by no means I may discover them   75
By any mark of favor.
Brutus.   Let 'em enter.
They are the faction. O Conspiracy,
Sham'st thou to show thy dang'rous brow by night,
When evils are most free? O then, by day
Where wilt thou find a cavern dark enough   80
To mask thy monstrous visage? Seek none, Con-
    spiracy,
Hide it in smiles and affability,
For if thou path, thy native semblance on,
Not Erebus itself were dim enough
To hide thee from prevention.   85

*Enter the conspirators, Cassius, Casca, Decius,
    Cinna, Metellus, and Trebonius.*

66–9 The genius . . . insurrection N. 70 brother Cassius was
married to Junia, Brutus' sister. 72 moe more (in number).
75 discover find out their identities. 76 mark of favor distinctive
feature. 83 path walk abroad. native semblance natural face.
84 Erebus the dark region leading to Hades. 85 prevention being
forestalled.

Cassius. I think we are too bold upon your rest.
Good morrow, Brutus; do we trouble you?

Brutus. I have been up this hour, awake all night.
Know I these men that come along with you?　　　89

Cassius. Yes, every man of them; and no man here
But honors you; and every one doth wish
You had but that opinion of yourself
Which every noble Roman bears of you.
This is Trebonius.

Brutus. He is welcome hither.　　　95

Cassius. This, Decius Brutus.

Brutus. He is welcome too.

Cassius. This, Casca; this, Cinna; and this, Metellus
　　Cimber.

Brutus. They are all welcome.
What watchful cares do interpose themselves　　　100
Betwixt your eyes and night?

Cassius. Shall I entreat a word?　　　*They whisper.*

Decius. Here lies the east; doth not the day break
　　here?

Casca. No.　　　104

Cinna. O pardon, sir, it doth, and yon grey lines
That fret the clouds are messengers of day.

Casca. You shall confess that you are both deceiv'd.
Here, as I point my sword, the sun arises,
Which is a great way growing on the south,
Weighing the youthful season of the year.　　　110
Some two months hence, up higher toward the north
He first presents his fire, and the high east
Stands, as the Capitol, directly here.

Brutus. Give me your hands all over, one by one.

86 **bold upon** bold in intruding upon. 106 **fret** interlace. 108 **as** where. 109 **growing on** encroaching on. 110 **Weighing** considering. 112 **high** exact.

Cassius. And let us swear our resolution.   115
  Brutus. No, not an oath. If not the face of men,
The sufferance of our souls, the time's abuse—
If these be motives weak, break off betimes,
And every man hence to his idle bed.
So let high-sighted tyranny range on,   120
Till each man drop by lottery. But if these,
As I am sure they do, bear fire enough
To kindle cowards and to steel with valor
The melting spirits of women, then, countrymen,
What need we any spur but our own cause   125
To prick us to redress? What other bond
Than secret Romans that have spoke the word
And will not palter? And what other oath
Than honesty to honesty engag'd,
That this shall be, or we will fall for it?   130
Swear priests and cowards, and men cautelous,
Old feeble carrions, and such suffering souls
That welcome wrongs. Unto bad causes swear
Such creatures as men doubt, but do not stain
The even virtue of our enterprise,   135
Nor th' insuppressive mettle of our spirits,
To think that or our cause or our performance
Did need an oath, when every drop of blood
That every Roman bears, and nobly bears,
Is guilty of a several bastardy,   140

115 **resolution** pronounced here with five syllables. 116 **face of men** men's apparent determination and honesty revealed in their looks. 117 **sufferance** suffering. 119 **idle** empty. 120 **high-sighted** N. 121 **lottery** chance. 126 **prick** urge. 127 **secret Romans** Romans who will remain quiet. 128 **palter** equivocate. 129 **honesty . . . engag'd** faith pledged to faith. 131 **cautelous** deceitful. 132 **carrions** dead bodies, i.e. soulless. 135 **even** uniform. 136 **insuppressive** insuppressible. 137 **or . . . or** either . . . or.
140 **several** separate. **bastardy** shows it is not truly Roman.

If he do break the smallest particle
Of any promise that hath pass'd from him.

Cassius. But what of Cicero? Shall we sound him?
I think he will stand very strong with us.   144

Casca. Let us not leave him out.

Cinna.   No, by no means.

Metellus. O let us have him, for his silver hairs
Will purchase us a good opinion
And buy men's voices to commend our deeds.
It shall be said his judgment rul'd our hands;
Our youths and wildness shall no whit appear,   150
But all be buried in his gravity.

Brutus. O name him not; let us not break with him,
For he will never follow anything
That other men begin.

Cassius.   Then leave him out.

Casca. Indeed, he is not fit.   155

Decius. Shall no man else be touch'd, but only
      Caesar?

Cassius. Decius, well urg'd. I think it is not meet
Mark Antony, so well belov'd of Caesar,
Should outlive Caesar; we shall find of him
A shrewd contriver. And you know his means,   160
If he improve them, may well stretch so far
As to annoy us all; which to prevent,
Let Antony and Caesar fall together.

Brutus. Our course will seem too bloody, Caius
      Cassius,
To cut the head off and then hack the limbs,   165

---

143 **sound him** find out his feelings on the matter. 150 **no whit**
not at all. 152 **break with** broach our plan to. 157 **urg'd** suggested.
160 **shrewd contriver** malicious planner. 161 **improve** make the
most of. 162 **annoy** harm.

30

Like wrath in death and envy afterwards;
For Antony is but a limb of Caesar.
Let's be sacrificers, but not butchers, Caius.
We all stand up against the spirit of Caesar,
And in the spirit of men there is no blood.   170
O that we then could come by Caesar's spirit,
And not dismember Caesar! But, alas,
Caesar must bleed for it. And, gentle friends,
Let's kill him boldly, but not wrathfully;
Let's carve him as a dish fit for the gods,   175
Not hew him as a carcass fit for hounds.
And let our hearts, as subtle masters do,
Stir up their servants to an act of rage,
And after seem to chide 'em. This shall make
Our purpose necessary and not envious;   180
Which so appearing to the common eyes,
We shall be call'd purgers, not murderers.
And for Mark Antony, think not of him,
For he can do no more than Caesar's arm
When Caesar's head is off.
   Cassius.   Yet I fear him,   185
For in the ingrafted love he bears to Caesar—
  Brutus. Alas, good Cassius, do not think of him.
If he love Caesar, all that he can do
Is to himself take thought and die for Caesar.
And that were much he should, for he is given   190
To sports, to wildness, and much company.
  Trebonius. There is no fear in him; let him not die,

166 **wrath . . . afterwards** would make it seem that we killed
him out of malice. 171 **come by** possess. 173 **gentle** noble. 175
carve cut up ceremoniously. 177 **subtle** cunning. 178 **servants**
the passions. 182 **purgers** healers. 186 **ingrafted** deep rooted.
189 **take thought** ponder. 190 **And . . . should** more than he will
probably do. 192 **fear** cause for fear. **in** from.

For he will live, and laugh at this hereafter.
                                        Clock strikes.
Brutus. Peace, count the clock.
Cassius.   The clock hath stricken three.
Trebonius. 'Tis time to part.
Cassius.   But it is doubtful yet
Whether Caesar will come forth today or no;   196
For he is superstitious grown of late,
Quite from the main opinion he held once
Of fantasy, of dreams, and ceremonies.
It may be these apparent prodigies,   200
The unaccustom'd terror of this night,
And the persuasion of his augurers
May hold him from the Capitol today.
  Decius. Never fear that. If he be so resolv'd,
I can o'ersway him, for he loves to hear   205
That unicorns may be betray'd with trees,
And bears with glasses, elephants with holes,
Lions with toils, and men with flatterers.
But when I tell him he hates flatterers,
He says, he does, being then most flattered.   210
Let me work,
For I can give his humor the true bent,
And I will bring him to the Capitol.
  Cassius. Nay, we will all of us be there to fetch him.
  Brutus. By the eight hour, is that the uttermost?
  Cinna. Be that the uttermost, and fail not then. 216

193 SD **Clock strikes** N. 196 **Whether** read 'whe'er.' 198 **from . . .
opinion** changed from the strong conviction. 199 **fantasy** fancy.
ceremonies omens. 200 **apparent** manifest. 206 **trees** by luring
them to drive their single horn into a tree. 207 **glasses** mirrors
(to blind them). **holes** pitfalls. 208 **toils** nets. 212 **give . . . bent**
shape his disposition in the right direction. 215 **eight** eighth.
uttermost latest.

Metellus. Caius Ligarius doth bear Caesar hard,
Who rated him for speaking well of Pompey.
I wonder none of you have thought of him.
  Brutus. Now, good Metellus, go along by him; 220
He loves me well, and I have given him reasons;
Send him but hither, and I'll fashion him.
  Cassius. The morning comes upon's; we'll leave you,
    Brutus,
And, friends, disperse yourselves, but all remember
What you have said, and show yourselves true
    Romans. 225
  Brutus. Good gentlemen, look fresh and merrily;
Let not our looks put on our purposes,
But bear it as our Roman actors do,
With untir'd spirits and formal constancy.
And so good morrow to you every one. 230
                    Exeunt. Manet Brutus.

          ! Fast asleep? It is no matter;
          oney-heavy dew of slumber.
          o figures nor no fantasies
          care draws in the brains of men;
          ou sleep'st so sound.

              Enter Portia.

                    Brutus, my lord.
          tia, what mean you? Wherefore rise you
                              236

          your health thus to commit
          ndition to the raw, cold morning.

          d. 220 by him by his house. 222 fashion persuade.
          urposes show our intentions. 228 bear it carry it
          constancy dignified and unchanging demeanor.
          es, pictures.

                              33

Martha

Portia. Nor for yours neither. Y' have ungently,
Brutus,
Stole from my bed; and yesternight at supper   240
You suddenly arose, and walk'd about,
Musing and sighing, with your arms across,
And when I ask'd you what the matter was,
You star'd upon me with ungentle looks.   244
I urg'd you further; then you scratch'd your head,
And too impatiently stamp'd with your foot;
Yet I insisted, yet you answer'd not,
But with an angry wafter of your hand
Gave sign for me to leave you. So I did,
Fearing to strengthen that impatience   250
Which seem'd too much enkindled, and withal
Hoping it was but an effect of humor,
Which sometime hath his hour with every man.
It will not let you eat, nor talk, nor sleep,
And could it work so much upon your shape   255
As it hath much prevail'd on your condition,
I should not know you Brutus. Dear my lord,
Make me acquainted with your cause of grief.
    Brutus. I am not well in health, and that is all.   259
    Portia. Brutus is wise, and were he not in health,
He would embrace the means to come by it.
    Brutus. Why, so I do. Good Portia, go to bed.
    Portia. Is Brutus sick, and is it physical
To walk unbraced and suck up the humors
Of the dank morning? What, is Brutus sick,   265

242 **arms across** folded in contemplative pose. 248 **wafter** wave.
250 **impatience** pronounced here with four syllables. 251 **withal**
moreover. 252 **humor** mood. 253 **his** its. 256 **condition** state of
mind. 257 **know you Brutus** recognize you as Brutus. 261 **come
by** achieve. 263 **physical** medicinal. 264 **unbraced** with doublet
open. **humors** dampness.

34

And will he steal out of his wholesome bed
To dare the vile contagion of the night,
And tempt the rheumy and unpurged air
To add unto his sickness? No, my Brutus,
You have some sick offense within your mind,   270
Which, by the right and virtue of my place,
I ought to know of; and, upon my knees,
I charm you, by my once-commended beauty,
By all your vows of love, and that great vow
Which did incorporate and make us one,   275
That you unfold to me, your self, your half,
Why you are heavy, and what men tonight
Have had resort to you; for here have been
Some six or seven who did hide their faces
Even from darkness.
  Brutus.   Kneel not, gentle **Portia.**   280
  Portia. I should not need, if you were gentle **Brutus.**
Within the bond of marriage, tell me, **Brutus,**
Is it excepted I should know no secrets
That appertain to you? Am I yourself
But, as it were, in sort or limitation,   285
To keep with you at meals, comfort your bed,
And talk to you sometimes? Dwell I but in the
    suburbs
Of your good pleasure? If it be no more,
Portia is Brutus' harlot, not his wife.
  Brutus. You are my true and honorable wife,   290
As dear to me as are the ruddy drops
That visit my sad heart.

268 **tempt** risk. **rheumy** causing rheum or catarrh. **unpurged**
unpurified by the sun. 270 **sick offense** sickness that troubles.
273 **charm** conjure, entreat. 277 **heavy** depressed. 285 **in . . .**
limitation only after a fashion or with limitations. 287 **suburbs**
outskirts, the London bawdy houses were in the suburbs.

Portia. If this were true, then should I know this
    secret.
I grant I am a woman, but, withal,
A woman that Lord Brutus took to wife;   295
I grant I am a woman, but, withal,
A woman well reputed, Cato's daughter.
Think you I am no stronger than my sex,
Being so father'd and so husbanded?
Tell me your counsels, I will not disclose 'em.   300
I have made strong proof of my constancy,
Giving myself a voluntary wound,
Here, in the thigh; can I bear that with patience
And not my husband's secrets?
    Brutus.   O ye gods!   304
Render me worthy of this noble wife!   *Knock.*
Hark, hark, one knocks. Portia, go in awhile,
And by and by thy bosom shall partake
The secrets of my heart.
All my engagements I will construe to thee,
All the charactery of my sad brows.   310
Leave me with haste.   *Exit Portia.*

Enter Lucius and Ligarius.

                    Lucius, who's that knocks?
Lucius. Here is a sick man that would speak with
    you.
Brutus. Caius Ligarius, that Metellus spake of.
Boy, stand aside. Caius Ligarius, how?

297 **Cato** Marcus Porcius Cato, a stern and uncompromising
republican who killed himself rather than submit to Caesar.
302 **wound** N. 309 **engagements** acts I am committed to. **construe**
explain. 310 **charactery** (stressed — ‿́ — ‿́) literally, hand-
writing; Brutus is using the figure here of himself as teacher
translating the language of his face.
    36

Caius. Vouchsafe good morrow from a feeble
    tongue.   315
Brutus. O what a time have you chose out, brave
    Caius,
To wear a kerchief! Would you were not sick.
  Caius. I am not sick if Brutus have in hand
Any exploit worthy the name of honor.   319
  Brutus. Such an exploit have I in hand, Ligarius,
Had you a healthful ear to hear of it.
  Caius. By all the gods that Romans bow before,
I here discard my sickness. Soul of Rome,
Brave son deriv'd from honorable loins,
Thou, like an exorcist, hast conjur'd up   325
My mortified spirit. Now bid me run,
And I will strive with things impossible;
Yea, get the better of them. What's to do?
  Brutus. A piece of work that will make sick men
    whole.
  Caius. But are not some whole that we must make
    sick?   330
  Brutus. That must we also. What it is, my Caius,
I shall unfold to thee as we are going
To whom it must be done.
  Caius.   Set on your foot,
And with a heart new fir'd I follow you,
To do I know not what; but it sufficeth   335
That Brutus leads me on.   *Thunder.*
  Brutus.   Follow me then.   *Exeunt.*

---

315 **Vouchsafe** deign to accept. 317 **kerchief** cloth around the
head of the sick man. 325 **exorcist** one who drives out evil spirits
326 **mortified** diseased. 329 **whole** well. 333 Set . . . **foot** proceed.

SCENE 2

*Thunder and lightning. Enter Julius Caesar in his
nightgown.*

Caesar. Nor heaven nor earth have been at peace
  tonight:
Thrice hath Calpurnia in her sleep cried out,
'Help, ho! They murther Caesar!' Who's within?

Enter a Servant.

Servant. My lord.
Caesar. Go bid the priests do present sacrifice,   5
And bring me their opinions of success.
Servant. I will, my lord.   *Exit.*

Enter Calpurnia.

Calpurnia. What mean you, Caesar? Think you to
  walk forth?
You shall not stir out of your house today.
Caesar. Caesar shall forth. The things that treat-
  en'd me   10
Ne'er look'd but on my back; when they shall see
The face of Caesar, they are vanished.
Calpurnia. Caesar, I never stood on ceremonies,
Yet now they fright me. There is one within,
Besides the things that we have heard and seen,   15
Recounts most horrid sights seen by the watch.
A lioness hath whelped in the streets;

SD **nightgown** robe. **3 murther** old spelling and pronunciation of
'murder.' **5 present** immediate. **13 stood on ceremonies** believed
in omens or augury. **16 watch** the night patrol.

And graves have yawn'd and yielded up their dead;
Fierce fiery warriors fought upon the clouds,
In ranks and squadrons and right form of war,   20
Which drizel'd blood upon the Capitol;
The noise of battle hurtled in the air,
Horses did neigh, and dying men did groan,
And ghosts did shriek and squeal about the streets.
O Caesar, these things are beyond all use,   25
And I do fear them.
   Caesar.   What can be avoided
Whose end is purpos'd by the mighty gods?
Yet Caesar shall go forth, for these predictions
Are to the world in general as to Caesar.
   Calpurnia. When beggars die there are no comets
      seen;   30
The heavens themselves blaze forth the death of
      princes.
   Caesar. Cowards die many times before their deaths,
The valiant never taste of death but once.
Of all the wonders that I yet have heard,   34
It seems to me most strange that men should fear,
Seeing that death, a necessary end,
Will come, when it will come.

           Enter a Servant.

                 What say the augurers?
   Servant. They would not have you to stir forth
      today.
Plucking the entrails of an offering forth,
They could not find a heart within the beast.   40

20 **right form of war** regular military formation. 22 **hurtled** clashed, made a din. 25 **use** normality. 27 **purpos'd** destined. 28 **Yet** nonetheless. 29 **Are to** bear as much on. 31 **blaze forth** proclaim.

Caesar. The gods do this in shame of cowardice:
Caesar should be a beast without a heart
If he should stay at home today for fear.
No, Caesar shall not; Danger knows full well
That Caesar is more dangerous than he.   45
We are two lions litter'd in one day,
And I the elder and more terrible,
And Caesar shall go forth.
    Calpurnia.   Alas, my lord,
Your wisdom is consum'd in confidence.
Do not go forth today. Call it my fear   50
That keeps you in the house, and not your own.
We'll send Mark Antony to the Senate House,
And he shall say you are not well today.
Let me, upon my knee, prevail in this.   54
    Caesar. Mark Antony shall say I am not well,
And, for thy humor, I will stay at home.

Enter Decius.

Here's Decius Brutus, he shall tell them so.
    Decius. Caesar, all hail! Good morrow, worthy
        Caesar,
I come to fetch you to the Senate House.
    Caesar. And you are come in very happy time   60
To bear my greeting to the senators
And tell them that I will not come today.
Cannot, is false, and that I dare not, falser.
I will not come today, tell them so, Decius.   64
    Calpurnia. Say he is sick.
    Caesar.   Shall Caesar send a lie?
Have I in conquest stretch'd mine arm so far
To be afear'd to tell greybeards the truth?
Decius, go tell them Caesar will not come.

42 should would. 46 We are N. 56 humor whim.
40

Decius. Most mighty Caesar, let me know some
    cause,
Lest I be laugh'd at when I tell them so.   70
  Caesar. The cause is in my will, I will not come.
That is enough to satisfy the Senate,
But for your private satisfaction,
Because I love you, I will let you know.
Calpurnia here, my wife, stays me at home.   75
She dreamt tonight she saw my statue,
Which, like a fountain with a hundred spouts,
Did run pure blood, and many lusty Romans
Came smiling and did bathe their hands in it.   79
And these does she apply for warnings, and portents,
And evils imminent; and on her knee
Hath begg'd that I will stay at home today.
  Decius. This dream is all amiss interpreted;
It was a vision fair and fortunate:
Your statue spouting blood in many pipes,   85
In which so many smiling Romans bath'd,
Signifies that from you great Rome shall suck
Reviving blood, and that great men shall press
For tinctures, stains, relics, and cognizance.
This by Calpurnia's dream is signified.   90
  Caesar. And this way have you well expounded it.
  Decius. I have, when you have heard what I can
    say;
And know it now, the Senate have concluded
To give this day a crown to mighty Caesar.
If you shall send them word you will not come, 95
Their minds may change. Besides, it were a mock

73 **satisfaction** five syllables here. 75 **stays** keeps. 76 **statue** trisyllabic, read 'stat-u-a.' 88 **press** crowd. 89 **tinctures . . . cognizance** N. 96 **mock** gibe.

Apt to be render'd, for some one to say,
'Break up the Senate till another time,
When Caesar's wife shall meet with better dreams.'
If Caesar hide himself, shall they not whisper,   100
'Lo, Caesar is afraid.'
Pardon me, Caesar, for my dear dear love
To your proceeding bids me tell you this,
And reason to my love is liable.
  Caesar. How foolish do your fears seem now,
    Calpurnia!   105
I am ashamed I did yield to them.
Give me my robe, for I will go.

Enter Brutus, Ligarius, Metellus, Casca, Trebonius,
Cinna, and Publius.

And look where Publius is come to fetch me.
  Publius. Good morrow, Caesar.
  Caesar.   Welcome, Publius.
What, Brutus, are you stirr'd so early too?   110
Good morrow, Casca. Caius Ligarius,
Caesar was ne'er so much your enemy
As that same ague which hath made you lean.
What is't o'clock?
  Brutus.   Caesar, 'tis strucken eight.   114
  Caesar. I thank you for your pains and courtesy.

Enter Antony.

See, Antony, that revels long a'nights,
Is notwithstanding up. Good morrow, Antony.
  Antony. So to most noble Caesar.

---

97 **Apt . . . render'd** likely to be made. 103 **proceeding** advancement. 104 **liable** subservient. 108 **fetch** escort. 114 **What . . . o'clock?** what time is it?
42

Caesar. Bid them prepare within.
I am to blame to be thus waited for.
Now, Cinna, now, Metellus; what, Trebonius,   120
I have an hour's talk in store for you;
Remember that you call on me today;
Be near me, that I may remember you.
  Trebonius. Caesar, I will [*Aside.*] and so near will
    I be   124
That your best friends shall wish I had been further.
  Caesar. Good friends, go in and taste some wine
    with me,
And we, like friends, will straightway go together.
  Brutus. [*Aside.*] That every like is not the same, O
    Caesar,   128
The heart of Brutus earns to think upon.   *Exeunt.*

Enter Artemidorus.

Artemidorus. 'Caesar, beware of Brutus; take heed
of Cassius, come not near Casca, have an eye to
Cinna, trust not Trebonius, mark well Metellus Cimber, Decius Brutus loves thee not, thou hast wrong'd
Caius Ligarius. There is but one mind in all these
men, and it is bent against Caesar. If thou beest not
immortal, look about you. Security gives way to
conspiracy. The mighty gods defend thee.   137
                Thy lover, ARTEMIDORUS.'
Here will I stand till Caesar pass along,
And as a suitor will I give him this.   140
My heart laments that virtue cannot live

---

128 **That . . . same** that to be like friends is not the same as
being friends. 129 **earns** grieves. SD **Enter Artemidorus** N. 136–7
Security . . . conspiracy unguardedness opens a way to conspiracy.

Out of the teeth of emulation.
If thou read this, O Caesar, thou mayest live;
If not, the Fates with traitors do contrive.   *Exit.*

Enter Portia and Lucius.

Portia. I prithee, boy, run to the Senate House;
Stay not to answer me, but get thee gone.   146
Why dost thou stay?
     Lucius.   To know my errand, madam.
     Portia. I would have had thee there, and here again
Ere I can tell thee what thou shouldst do there.
O constancy, be strong upon my side;   150
Set a huge mountain 'tween my heart and tongue;
I have a man's mind, but a woman's might:
How hard it is for women to keep counsel.
Art thou here yet?
     Lucius.   Madam, what should I do?
Run to the Capitol, and nothing else?   155
And so return to you, and nothing else?
     Portia. Yes, bring me word, boy, if thy lord look
          well,
For he went sickly forth; and take good note
What Caesar doth, what suitors press to him.
Hark, boy, what noise is that?   160
     Lucius. I hear none, madam.
     Portia.   Prithee, listen well:
I heard a bustling rumor, like a fray,
And the wind brings it from the Capitol.
     Lucius. Sooth, madam, I hear nothing.

Enter the Soothsayer.

142 **Out . . . emulation** (five syllables) free from the biting of
envy. 144 **contrive** work. 150 **constancy** self-possession. 162 **bustling rumor** noisy tumult. 164 **Sooth** in truth.

Portia. Come hither, fellow; which way hast thou
  been? 165
Soothsayer. At mine own house, good lady.
Portia. What is't o'clock?
Soothsayer.   About the ninth hour, lady.
Portia. Is Caesar yet gone to the Capitol?
Soothsayer. Madam, not yet, I go to take my stand
To see him pass on to the Capitol. 170
Portia. Thou hast some suit to Caesar, hast thou
  not?
Soothsayer. That I have, lady, if it will please
  Caesar
To be so good to Caesar as to hear me,
I shall beseech him to befriend himself.
Portia. Why, know'st thou any harm's intended
  towards him? 175
Soothsayer. None that I know will be, much that I
  fear may chance.
Good morrow to you. Here the street is narrow;
The throng that follows Caesar at the heels
Of senators, of praetors, common suitors,
Will crowd a feeble man almost to death. 180
I'll get me to a place more void, and there
Speak to great Caesar as he comes along.
Portia. I must go in. Ay me. How weak a thing
The heart of woman is! O Brutus,
The heavens speed thee in thine enterprise. 185
Sure, the boy heard me—Brutus hath a suit
That Caesar will not grant—O, I grow faint—
Run, Lucius, and commend me to my lord.
Say I am merry. Come to me again,
And bring me word what he doth say to thee. 190
                                    Exeunt.

181 **void** open. 189 **merry** in good spirits.

45

Act III

Flourish.

Enter Caesar, Brutus, Cassius, Casca, Decius, Metellus, Trebonius, Cinna, Antony, Lepidus, Artemidorus, Publius, [Popilius,] and Soothsayer.

Caesar. The ides of March are come.
Soothsayer. Ay, Caesar, but not gone.
Artemidorus. Hail, Caesar! Read this schedule.
Decius. Trebonius doth desire you to o'er-read,
At your best leisure, this his humble suit.   5
Artemidorus. O Caesar, read mine first, for mine's
  a suit
That touches Caesar nearer. Read it, great Caesar.
Caesar. What touches us ourself shall be last serv'd.
Artemidorus. Delay not, Caesar, read it instantly.
Caesar. What, is the fellow mad?   10
Publius. Sirrah, give place.
Cassius. What, urge you your petitions in the
  street?
Come to the Capitol.
Popilius. I wish your enterprise today may thrive.
Cassius. What enterprise, Popilius?   15
Popilius. Fare you well.

3 **schedule** scroll. 11 **give place** make room.
  46

Brutus. What said Popilius Lena?
Cassius. He wish'd today our enterprise might
    thrive:
I fear our purpose is discovered.   19
  Brutus. Look, how he makes to Caesar: mark him.
  Cassius. Casca, be sudden, for we fear prevention.
Brutus, what shall be done? If this be known,
Cassius or Caesar never shall turn back,
For I will slay myself.
  Brutus. Cassius, be constant: 25
Popilius Lena speaks not of our purposes,
For, look, he smiles, and Caesar doth not change.
  Cassius. Trebonius knows his time, for, look you,
    Brutus,
He draws Mark Antony out of the way.
  Decius. Where is Metellus Cimber? Let him go   30
And presently prefer his suit to Caesar.
  Brutus. He is address'd; press near and second him.
  Cinna. Casca, you are the first that rears your
    hand.
  Caesar. Are we all ready? What is now amiss
That Caesar and his Senate must redress?   35
  Metellus. Most high, most mighty, and most puis-
    sant Caesar,
Metellus Cimber throws before thy seat
An humble heart—
  Caesar.   I must prevent thee, Cimber.
These couchings and these lowly courtesies
Might fire the blood of ordinary men   40
And turn preordinance and first decree

20 makes to goes toward. 21 sudden quick. 25 constant firm in
purpose. 31 prefer plead. 32 address'd ready. 36 puissant power-
ful. 39 couchings obeisances. courtesies bows. 41 preordinance
. . . decree the preordained and unchanging law.
                      47

Into the law of children. Be not fond
To think that Caesar bears such rebel blood
That will be thaw'd from the true quality   44
With that which melteth fools; I mean sweet words,
Low-crooked curtsies, and base spaniel fawning.
Thy brother by decree is banished.
If thou dost bend, and pray, and fawn for him,
I spurn thee like a cur out of my way.   49
Know, Caesar doth not wrong, nor without cause
Will he be satisfied.
   Metellus. Is there no voice more worthy than my
     own,
To sound more sweetly in great Caesar's ear
For the repealing of my banish'd brother?   54
   Brutus. I kiss thy hand, but not in flattery, Caesar;
Desiring thee that Publius Cimber may
Have an immediate freedom of repeal.
   Caesar. What, Brutus!
   Cassius.   Pardon, Caesar; Caesar, pardon.
As low as to thy foot doth Cassius fall,
To beg enfranchisement for Publius Cimber.   60
   Caesar. I could be well mov'd if I were as you;
If I could pray to move, prayers would move me.
But I am constant as the northern star,
Of whose true-fix'd and resting quality

42 **law of children** caprice and uncertainty. **fond** (so) foolish (as).
43 **rebel blood** ungovernable passions. 45 **With that** by those
things. 46 **Low-crooked** low-bent. **curtsies** bows, a syncopated
form of *courtesies*. **spaniel** obsequious, doglike. 50–1 **Caesar . . .
satisfied** N. 54 **repealing** recalling (from exile). 57 **freedom of
repeal** pardon to be recalled. 61–2 **I could . . . me** If I were as
weak as you I could be made to change my mind, and if I could
ask others to change their minds, then I could change. **well** very
likely. 64 **resting** stable.

48

There is no fellow in the firmament.   65
The skies are painted with unnumber'd sparks;
They are all fire and every one doth shine,
But there's but one in all doth hold his place.
So, in the world: 'tis furnish'd well with men,
And men are flesh and blood, and apprehensive;   70
Yet in the number, I do know but one
That unassailable holds on his rank,
Unshak'd of motion, and that I am he
Let me a little show it, even in this:
That I was constant Cimber should be banish'd,   75
And constant do remain to keep him so.
  Cinna. O Caesar.
  Caesar. Hence! Wilt thou lift up Olympus?
  Decius. Great Caesar.
  Caesar. Doth not Brutus bootless kneel?   80
  Casca. Speak, hands, for me.

They stab Caesar.

  Caesar. Et tu, Brute?—Then fall, Caesar!   *Dies.*
  Cinna. Liberty! Freedom! Tyranny is dead!
Run hence, proclaim, cry it about the streets.   84
  Cassius. Some to the common pulpits, and cry out
Liberty, freedom, and enfranchisement.
  Brutus. People and senators, be not affrighted.
Fly not, stand still; ambition's debt is paid.
  Casca. Go to the pulpit, Brutus.
  Decius.   And Cassius too.

65 **firmament** heavens. 66 **painted** decorated. **unnumber'd** innumerable. 70 **apprehensive** capable of reasoning. 72 **holds . . . rank** maintains his position. 73 **of motion** by prompting, either inward or outward. 78 **Olympus** the mountain home of the Greek gods. 80 **bootless** unavailingly. 85 **common pulpits** public platforms for delivering speeches, *rostra.*

Brutus. Where's Publius?   90
Cinna. Here, quite confounded with this mutiny.
Metellus. Stand fast together, lest some friend of
     Caesar's
Should chance—
Brutus. Talk not of standing. Publius, good cheer;
There is no harm intended to your person,   95
Nor to no Roman else; so tell them, Publius.
Cassius. And leave us, Publius, lest that the people,
Rushing on us, should do your age some mischief.
Brutus. Do so; and let no man abide this deed
But we the doers.   100

Enter Trebonius.

Cassius. Where is Antony?
Trebonius.   Fled to his house amaz'd.
Men, wives, and children stare, cry out, and run,
As it were doomsday.
Brutus.   Fates, we will know your pleasures.
That we shall die, we know; 'tis but the time
And drawing days out that men stand upon.   105
Casca. Why, he that cuts off twenty years of life
Cuts off so many years of fearing death.
Brutus. Grant that, and then is death a benefit.
So are we Caesar's friends, that have abridg'd   109
His time of fearing death. Stoop, Romans, stoop,
And let us bathe our hands in Caesar's blood
Up to the elbows, and besmear our swords.
Then walk we forth, even to the market place,
And waving our red weapons o'er our heads,
Let's all cry, 'Peace, freedom, and liberty.'   115

91 **mutiny** discord. 99 **abide** pay for. 101 **amaz'd** utterly confounded. 102 **wives** women. 105 **stand upon** are concerned for.
113 **even** read 'e'en.'

Cassius. Stoop then, and wash. How many ages
    hence
Shall this our lofty scene be acted over,
In states unborn and accents yet unknown!
   Brutus. How many times shall Caesar bleed in
    sport,
That now on Pompey's basis lies along,   120
No worthier than the dust?
   Cassius.   So oft as that shall be,
So often shall the knot of us be call'd
The men that gave their country liberty.
   Decius. What, shall we forth?
   Cassius.   Ay, every man away.
Brutus shall lead, and we will grace his heels   125
With the most boldest and best hearts of Rome.

Enter a Servant.

   Brutus. Soft, who comes here? A friend of
    Antony's.
   Servant. Thus, Brutus, did my master bid me kneel,
Thus did Mark Antony bid me fall down,
And being prostrate, thus he bade me say: 130
Brutus is noble, wise, valiant, and honest;
Caesar was mighty, bold, royal, and loving.
Say I love Brutus, and I honor him;
Say I fear'd Caesar, honor'd him, and lov'd him.
If Brutus will vouchsafe that Antony   135
May safely come to him, and be resolv'd
How Caesar hath deserv'd to lie in death,
Mark Antony shall not love Caesar dead
So well as Brutus living, but will follow

118 **accents** languages. 120 **Pompey's basis** the base of Pompey's
statue. 122 **knot** group. 131 **honest** honorable. 136 **resolv'd**
informed.

The fortunes and affairs of noble Brutus   140
Thorough the hazards of this untrod state
With all true faith. So says my master Antony.

Brutus. Thy master is a wise and valiant **Roman,**
I never thought him worse.
Tell him, so please him come unto this place,   145
He shall be satisfied, and by my honor
Depart untouch'd.

Servant. I'll fetch him presently.   *Exit Servant.*

Brutus. I know that we shall have him well to friend.

Cassius. I wish we may, but yet have I a mind   150
That fears him much, and my misgiving still
Falls shrewdly to the purpose.

Enter Antony.

Brutus. But here comes Antony. Welcome, **Mark**
Antony.

Antony. O mighty Caesar! Dost thou lie so low?
Are all thy conquests, glories, triumphs, spoils,   155
Shrunk to this little measure? Fare thee well.
I know not, gentlemen, what you intend,
Who else must be let blood, who else is rank.
If I myself, there is no hour so fit
As Caesar's death hour, nor no instrument   160
Of half that worth as those your swords, made **rich**
With the most noble blood of all this world.
I do beseech ye, if you bear me hard,
Now, whilst your purpled hands do reek **and smoke,**

141 **Thorough** (two syllables) throughout. 145 **so . . . come** if
it pleases him to come. 148 **presently** immediately. 151–2 **still . . .
purpose** always proves well grounded. 152 **shrewdly** 'dangerously'
close. 158 **let blood** bled (for reasons of health). **rank** sick.
163 **bear me hard** bear a grudge against me. 164 **purpled** dyed
crimson.

Fulfill your pleasure. Live a thousand years,   165
I shall not find myself so apt to die.
No place will please me so, no mean of death,
As here by Caesar, and by you cut off,
The choice and master spirits of this age.
  Brutus. O Antony! Beg not your death of us.   170
Though now we must appear bloody and cruel,
As by our hands and this our present act
You see we do, yet see you but our hands
And this, the bleeding business they have done.
Our hearts you see not, they are pitiful;   175
And pity to the general wrong of Rome—
As fire drives out fire, so pity pity—
Hath done this deed on Caesar. For your part,
To you our swords have leaden points, Mark
    Antony:
Our arms in strength of malice, and our hearts   180
Of brothers' temper, do receive you in
With all kind love, good thoughts, and reverence.
  Cassius. Your voice shall be as strong as any man's
In the disposing of new dignities.
  Brutus. Only be patient, till we have appeas'd   185
The multitude, beside themselves with fear,
And then we will deliver you the cause
Why I, that did love Caesar when I strook him,
Have thus proceeded.
  Antony.   I doubt not of your wisdom.
Let each man render me his bloody hand.   190
First, Marcus Brutus, will I shake with you;

165 **Live** if I live. 166 **apt** ready. 167 **mean** manner, means.
180 **in . . . malice** the arms of the conspirators are still covered
with blood. **malice** enmity. 184 **disposing . . . dignities** dis-
tributing new positions. 187 **deliver** tell. 188 **strook** older form of
'struck.'

Next, Caius Cassius, do I take your hand;
Now, Decius Brutus, yours; now yours, Metellus;
Yours, Cinna; and, my valiant Casca, yours;   194
Though last, not least in love, yours, good Trebonius
Gentlemen all; alas, what shall I say?
My credit now stands on such slippery ground
That one of two bad ways you must conceit me,
Either a coward or a flatterer.
That I did love thee, Caesar, O 'tis true;   200
If then thy spirit look upon us now,
Shall it not grieve thee dearer than thy death
To see thy Antony making his peace,
Shaking the bloody fingers of thy foes?
Most noble, in the presence of thy corse!   205
Had I as many eyes as thou hast wounds,
Weeping as fast as they stream forth thy blood,
It would become me better than to close
In terms of friendship with thine enemies.   209
Pardon me, Julius; here wast thou bay'd, brave hart
Here didst thou fall, and here thy hunters stand,
Sign'd in thy spoil, and crimson'd in thy Lethe.
O world, thou wast the forest to this hart,
And this, indeed, O world, the hart of thee.
How like a deer, stroken by many princes,   215
Dost thou here lie!
  Cassius. Mark Antony!
  Antony.   Pardon me, Caius Cassius.
The enemies of Caesar shall say this;

198 **conceit** understand, conceive. 202 **dearer** more keenly. 20
corse body. 208 **close** unite. 210 **bay'd** brought to bay. **hart** the
first of a series of puns on *hart*, a stag, and 'heart.' 212 **Sign'**
in thy spoil marked with your slaughter. **Lethe** river of death
i.e. lifeblood. 215 **stroken** struck down.

Then, in a friend, it is cold modesty.   219
  Cassius. I blame you not for praising Caesar so,
But what compact mean you to have with us?
Will you be prick'd in number of our friends,
Or shall we on, and not depend on you?
  Antony. Therefore I took your hands, but was in-
      deed   224
Sway'd from the point by looking down on Caesar.
Friends am I with you all, and love you all,
Upon this hope, that you shall give me reasons
Why and wherein Caesar was dangerous.
  Brutus. Or else were this a savage spectacle.
Our reasons are so full of good regard   230
That were you, Antony, the son of Caesar,
You should be satisfied.
  Antony.   That's all I seek,
And am moreover suitor that I may
Produce his body to the market place,
And in the pulpit, as becomes a friend,   235
Speak in the order of his funeral.
  Brutus. You shall, Mark Antony.
  Cassius.   Brutus, a word with you.
You know not what you do; do not consent
That Antony speak in his funeral.
Know you how much the people may be mov'd   240
By that which he will utter?
  Brutus.   By your pardon;
I will myself into the pulpit first
And show the reason of our Caesar's death.

---

219 **modesty** moderation. 221 **compact** (stressed — ´) agreement. 222 **prick'd in number** checked on the list. 223 **shall we on**
shall we proceed. 230 **good regard** what deserves approbation.
234 **Produce . . . to** show . . . in. 236 **order** proper ceremonies.

What Antony shall speak, I will protest
He speaks by leave and by permission,   245
And that we are contented Caesar shall
Have all true rites and lawful ceremonies.
It shall advantage more than do us wrong.
  Cassius. I know not what may fall, I like it not.
  Brutus. Mark Antony, here take you Caesar's body.
You shall not in your funeral speech blame us,   251
But speak all good you can devise of Caesar,
And say you do't by our permission;
Else shall you not have any hand at all
About his funeral. And you shall speak   255
In the same pulpit whereto I am going,   ·
After my speech is ended.
  Antony.   Be it so;
I do desire no more.
  Brutus. Prepare the body then, and follow us.   259
                          Exeunt. Manet Antony.
  Antony. O pardon me, thou bleeding piece of earth,
That I am meek and gentle with these butchers.
Thou art the ruins of the noblest man
That ever lived in the tide of times.
Woe to the hand that shed this costly blood.
Over thy wounds now do I prophesy,   265
Which like dumb mouths do ope their ruby lips
To get the voice and utterance of my tongue,
A curse shall light upon the limbs of men:
Domestic fury and fierce civil strife
Shall cumber all the parts of Italy;   270
Blood and destruction shall be so in use,

---

244 **protest** proclaim. 245 **permission** four syllables here and in
l. 253 below. 249 **fall** happen. 263 **tide of times** ebb and flow of
time. 270 **cumber** burden. 271 **in use** customary.
    56

And dreadful objects so familiar,
That mothers shall but smile when they behold
Their infants quarter'd with the hands of war,
All pity chok'd with custom of fell deeds;   275
And Caesar's spirit, ranging for revenge,
With Ate by his side come hot from hell,
Shall in these confines with a monarch's voice
Cry 'Havoc,' and let slip the dogs of war,
That this foul deed shall smell above the earth   280
With carrion men groaning for burial.

Enter Octavius' Servant.

You serve Octavius Caesar, do you not?
  Servant. I do, Mark Antony.
  Antony. Caesar did write for him to come to Rome.
  Servant. He did receive his letters and is coming,
And bid me say to you by word of mouth—   286
O Caesar!
  Antony. Thy heart is big, get thee apart and weep.
Passion, I see, is catching, for mine eyes,
Seeing those beads of sorrow stand in thine,   290
Began to water. Is thy master coming?
  Servant. He lies tonight within seven leagues of
      Rome.
  Antony. Post back with speed and tell him what
      hath chanc'd.
Here is a mourning Rome, a dangerous Rome,
No Rome of safety for Octavius yet.   295

272 **familiar** four syllables here. 274 **quarter'd** cut up. 275 **custom**
commonness. **fell** cruel. 276 **ranging** searching. 277 **Ate** goddess
of discord. 279 **Havoc** the signal for 'no quarter.' **let slip** unleash.
288 **big** filled with sorrow. 289 **Passion** strong feeling, grief.
292 **lies** lodges. 295 **Rome** another pun based on the pronunciation 'room.'

Hie hence and tell him so. Yet, stay awhile;
Thou shalt not back till I have borne this corse
Into the market place; there shall I try,
In my oration, how the people take
The cruel issue of these bloody men;   300
According to the which, thou shalt discourse
To yong Octavius of the state of things.
Lend me your hand.   *Exeunt.*

SCENE 2

*Enter Brutus and goes into the pulpit, and Cassius
with the Plebeians.*

Plebeians. We will be satisfied; let us be satisfied.

Brutus. Then follow me, and give me audience,
    friends.
Cassius, go you into the other street,
And part the numbers.   4
Those that will hear me speak, let 'em stay here;
Those that will follow Cassius, go with him,
And public reasons shall be rendred
Of Caesar's death.

1. Plebeian.   I will hear Brutus speak.

2. Plebeian. I will hear Cassius, and compare their
    reasons,
When severally we hear them rendred.   10

3. Plebeian. The noble Brutus is ascended: silence!

Brutus. Be patient till the last. Romans, countrymen, and lovers, hear me for my cause, and be silent,

300 **issue** deed. 302 **yong** young. 1 **satisfied** given satisfaction.
4 **part the numbers** divide the crowd. 7 **rendred** read 'rendered'
(three syllables). 10 **severally** separately. 12 **Be . . . last** wait
patiently until the last word. 13 **lovers** dear friends.

that you may hear. Believe me for mine honor, and have respect to mine honor, that you may believe. Censure me in your wisdom, and awake your senses, that you may the better judge. If there be any in this assembly, any dear friend of Caesar's, to him I say that Brutus' love to Caesar was no less than his. If then that friend demand why Brutus rose against Caesar, this is my answer: Not that I lov'd Caesar less, but that I lov'd Rome more. Had you rather Caesar were living, and die all slaves; than that Caesar were dead, to live all free men? As Caesar lov'd me, I weep for him; as he was fortunate, I rejoice at it; as he was valiant, I honor him; but, as he was ambitious, I slew him. There is tears, for his love; joy, for his fortune; honor, for his valor; and death, for his ambition. Who is here so base, that would be a bondman? If any, speak, for him have I offended. Who is here so rude, that would not be a Roman? If any, speak, for him have I offended. Who is here so vile, that will not love his country? If any, speak, for him have I offended. I pause for a reply.

All. None, Brutus, none. 35

Brutus. Then none have I offended. I have done no more to Caesar, than you shall do to Brutus. The question of his death is enroll'd in the Capitol; his glory not extenuated, wherein he was worthy, nor his offenses enforced, for which he suffered death.

Enter Mark Antony, with Caesar's body.

Here comes his body, mourn'd by Mark Antony, who,

15 have . . . honor remember that I am an honorable man. 16 Censure judge. senses powers of understanding. 31 rude uncivilized. 38 question topic of discussion. enroll'd recorded. 39 extenuated lessened. 40 enforced stressed.

though he had no hand in his death, shall receive the
benefit of his dying, a place in the commonwealth, as
which of you shall not? With this I depart: that, as
I slew my best lover for the good of Rome, I have the
same dagger for myself, when it shall please my
country to need my death.   47

All. Live, Brutus! live! live!

1. Plebeian. Bring him with triumph home unto his
house.   50

2. Plebeian. Give him a statue with his ancestors.

3. Plebeian. Let him be Caesar.

4. Plebeian. Caesar's better parts shall be **crown'd**
in Brutus.   54

1. Plebeian. We'll bring him to his house with
shouts and clamors.

Brutus. My countrymen.

2. Plebeian. Peace! silence! Brutus speaks.

1. Plebeian. Peace ho!   59

Brutus. Good countrymen, let me depart alone,
And, for my sake, stay here with Antony.
Do grace to Caesar's corpse, and grace his speech
Tending to Caesar's glories, which Mark Antony,
By our permission, is allow'd to make.
I do entreat you, not a man depart,   65
Save I alone, till Antony have spoke.   *Exit.*

1. Plebeian. Stay, ho! and let us hear Mark
Antony.

3. Plebeian. Let him go up into the public chair;
We'll hear him. Noble Antony, go up.   69

Antony. For Brutus' sake, I am beholding to you.

4. Plebeian. What does he say of Brutus?

43 place office, position. **54 parts** qualities. **70 beholding**
indebted.

60

3. Plebeian. He says, for Brutus' sake
He finds himself beholding to us all.

4. Plebeian. 'Twere best he speak no harm of
    Brutus here!

1. Plebeian. This Caesar was a tyrant.   75

3. Plebeian. Nay, that's certain.
We are bless'd that Rome is rid of him.

2. Plebeian. Peace, let us hear what Antony can
    say.

Antony. You gentle Romans—

All. Peace, ho, let us hear him.   80

Antony. Friends, Romans, countrymen, lend me
    your ears.
I come to bury Caesar, not to praise him.
The evil that men do lives after them,
The good is oft interred with their bones;
So let it be with Caesar. The noble Brutus   85
Hath told you Caesar was ambitious;
If it were so, it was a grievous fault,
And grievously hath Caesar answer'd it.
Here, under leave of Brutus and the rest—
For Brutus is an honorable man,   90
So are they all, all honorable men—
Come I to speak in Caesar's funeral.
He was my friend, faithful and just to me;
But Brutus says he was ambitious,
And Brutus is an honorable man.   95
He hath brought many captives home to Rome,
Whose ransoms did the general coffers fill.
Did this in Caesar seem ambitious?
When that the poor have cried, Caesar hath wept;
Ambition should be made of sterner stuff,   100

86 ambitious four syllables here and in ll. 94, 101, 106. 88 answer'd
paid for. 97 general coffers public treasury.

61

Yet Brutus says he was ambitious,
And Brutus is an honorable man.
You all did see that on the Lupercal
I thrice presented him a kingly crown,   104
Which he did thrice refuse. Was this ambition?
Yet Brutus says he was ambitious,
And, sure, he is an honorable man.
I speak not to disprove what Brutus spoke,
But here I am to speak what I do know.
You all did love him once, not without cause,   110
What cause withholds you then to mourn for him?
O judgment! thou art fled to brutish beasts,
And men have lost their reason. Bear with me,
My heart is in the coffin there with Caesar,
And I must pause, till it come back to me.   115

  1. Plebeian. Methinks there is much reason in his
    sayings.

  2. Plebeian. If thou consider rightly of the matter,
Caesar has had great wrong.

  3. Plebeian.   Has he, masters?
I fear there will a worse come in his place.

  4. Plebeian. Mark'd ye his words? He would not
    take the crown,   120
Therefore 'tis certain he was not ambitious.

  1. Plebeian. If it be found so, some will dear abide
    it.

  2. Plebeian. Poor soul, his eyes are red as fire with
    weeping.

  3. Plebeian. There's not a nobler man in Rome than
    Antony.

  4. Plebeian. Now mark him, he begins again to
    speak.   125

103 on the Lupercal on the day of the Lupercalia. 122 dear abide
pay heavily for it.

Antony. But yesterday, the word of Caesar might
Have stood against the world; now lies he there,
And none so poor to do him reverence.
O masters. If I were dispos'd to stir
Your hearts and minds to mutiny and rage,   130
I should do Brutus wrong, and Cassius wrong,
Who, you all know, are honorable men.
I will not do them wrong; I rather choose
To wrong the dead, to wrong myself and you,
Than I will wrong such honorable men.   135
But here's a parchment with the seal of Caesar;
I found it in his closet, 'tis his will.
Let but the commons hear this testament—
Which, pardon me, I do not mean to read—   139
And they would go and kiss dead Caesar's wounds,
And dip their napkins in his sacred blood,
Yea, beg a hair of him for memory,
And, dying, mention it within their wills,
Bequeathing it as a rich legacy
Unto their issue.   145
   4. Plebeian. We'll hear the will, read it, Mark
      Antony.
   All. The will, the will; we will hear Caesar's will.
   Antony. Have patience, gentle friends, I must not
      read it.
It is not meet you know how Caesar lov'd you;
You are not wood, you are not stones, but men,   150
And being men, hearing the will of Caesar,
It will inflame you, it will make you mad.
'Tis good you know not that you are his heirs,
For if you should, O what would come of it?   154

128 **none . . . reverence** there is none so poor as to show him
respect. 130 **mutiny** grow to disorder. 138 **commons** common
people. 141 **napkins** handkerchiefs.

4. Plebeian. Read the will, we'll hear it, Antony;
You shall read us the will, Caesar's will.

Antony. Will you be patient? Will you stay awhile?
I have o'ershot myself to tell you of it.
I fear I wrong the honorable men   159
Whose daggers have stabb'd Caesar; I do fear it.

4. Plebeian. They were traitors; honorable men?

All. The will, the testament!

2. Plebeian. They were villains, murderers. The
will! read the will!   164

Antony. You will compel me then to read the will;
Then make a ring about the corpse of Caesar,
And let me show you him that made the will.
Shall I descend? And will you give me leave?

All. Come down.

2. Plebeian. Descend.   170

3. Plebeian. You shall have leave.

4. Plebeian. A ring, stand round.

1. Plebeian. Stand from the hearse, stand from the
body.   174

2. Plebeian. Room for Antony, most noble Antony.

Antony. Nay, press not so upon me, stand far off.

All. Stand back! room! bear back!

Antony. If you have tears, prepare to shed them
        now.
You all do know this mantle; I remember
The first time ever Caesar put it on: 180
'Twas on a summer's evening, in his tent,
That day he overcame the Nervii.
Look, in this place ran Cassius' dagger through;
See what a rent the envious Casca made;
Through this, the well-beloved Brutus stabb'd,   185

158 o'ershot gone too far. 182 **Nervii** a Belgic tribe defeated by
Caesar in 57 B.C.

And as he pluck'd his cursed steel away,
Mark how the blood of Caesar followed it,
As rushing out of doors to be resolv'd
If Brutus so unkindly knock'd, or no;
For Brutus, as you know, was Caesar's angel.   190
Judge, O you gods, how dearly Caesar lov'd him.
This was the most unkindest cut of all.
For when the noble Caesar saw him stab,
Ingratitude, more strong than traitors' arms,   194
Quite vanquish'd him; then burst his mighty heart,
And in his mantle muffling up his face,
Even at the base of Pompey's statue,
Which all the while ran blood, great Caesar fell.
O, what a fall was there, my countrymen!
Then I, and you, and all of us fell down,   200
Whilst bloody treason flourish'd over us.
O now you weep, and I perceive you feel
The dint of pity; these are gracious drops.
Kind souls, what weep you when you but behold
Our Caesar's vesture wounded? Look you here!   205
Here is himself, marr'd as you see with traitors.
    1. Plebeian. O piteous spectacle!
    2. Plebeian. O noble Caesar!
    3. Plebeian. O woeful day!
    4. Plebeian. O traitors, villains!   210
    1. Plebeian. O most bloody sight!
    2. Plebeian. We will be reveng'd. Revenge!
About! Seek! Burn! Fire! Kill! Slay!
Let not a traitor live!

188 **to be resolv'd** to make certain. 189 **unkindly** both 'cruelly'
and 'unnaturally.' 190 **angel** dearest friend. 197 **statue** again
trisyllabic. 197–8 **Pompey's . . . blood** N. 203 **dint** blow, im-
pression. 206 **Here is himself** N. 213–14 **About . . . live** these
lines are usually given by editors to the entire mob to shout.

Antony. Stay, countrymen.   215

1. Plebeian. Peace there, hear the noble Antony.

2. Plebeian. We'll hear him, we'll follow him, we'll
die with him.

Antony. Good friends, sweet friends, let me not stir
you up

To such a sudden flood of mutiny.   220

They that have done this deed are honorable.

What private griefs they have, alas, I know not,

That made them do it; they are wise and honorable,

And will, no doubt, with reasons answer you.

I come not, friends, to steal away your hearts,   225

I am no orator, as Brutus is;

But, as you know me all, a plain blunt man,

That love my friend, and that they know full well,

That gave me public leave to speak of him.

For I have neither writ, nor words, nor worth,   230

Action, nor utterance, nor the power of speech,

To stir men's blood. I only speak right on;

I tell you that which you yourselves do know,

Show you sweet Caesar's wounds, poor, poor dumb
mouths,

And bid them speak for me. But were I Brutus,   235

And Brutus Antony, there were an Antony

Would ruffle up your spirits, and put a tongue

In every wound of Caesar, that should move

The stones of Rome to rise and mutiny.

All. We'll mutiny.   240

1. Plebeian. We'll burn the house of Brutus.

222 **griefs** grievances. 229 **public leave** leave to speak in public, a
transferred epithet. 230 **writ** prepared speech, formal oration.
231 **Action** gestures used by orator and actor to emphasize the
meaning of their words. **utterance** pronunciation, delivery. 232
right on with simple straightforwardness. 237 **ruffle** stir.

3. Plebeian. Away then! Come, seek the conspirators.

Antony. Yet hear me, countrymen; yet hear me
speak.

All. Peace ho! Hear Antony, most noble Antony!

Antony. Why friends, you go to do you know not
what.   245

Wherein hath Caesar thus deserv'd your loves?

Alas, you know not, I must tell you then:

You have forgot the will I told you of.

All. Most true, the will, let's stay and hear the will.

Antony. Here is the will, and under Caesar's seal.

To every Roman citizen he gives,   251

To every several man, seventy-five drachmas.

2. Plebeian. Most noble Caesar! We'll revenge his
death.

3. Plebeian. O royal Caesar!   255

Antony. Hear me with patience.

All. Peace, ho!

Antony. Moreover, he hath left you all his walks,

His private arbors, and new-planted orchards,

On this side Tiber; he hath left them you,   260

And to your heirs forever; common pleasures,

To walk abroad and recreate yourselves.

Here was a Caesar! When comes such another?

1. Plebeian. Never, never! Come, away, away!

We'll burn his body in the holy place,   265

And with the brands fire the traitors' houses.

Take up the body.

2. Plebeian. Go fetch fire.

3. Plebeian. Pluck down benches.   269

252 **several** individual. 259 **orchards** gardens. 261 **common
pleasures** public recreation grounds.

4. Plebeian. Pluck down forms, windows, anything.
Exeunt plebeians.

Antony. Now let it work: Mischief, thou art afoot,
Take thou what course thou wilt. How now fellow?

Enter Servant.

Servant. Sir, Octavius is already come to Rome.
Antony. Where is he?   274
Servant. He and Lepidus are at Caesar's house.
Antony. And thither will I straight to visit him.
He comes upon a wish. Fortune is merry,
And in this mood will give us anything.
Servant. I heard him say Brutus and Cassius   279
Are rid like madmen through the gates of Rome.
Antony. Belike they had some notice of the people,
How I had mov'd them. Bring me to Octavius.
Exeunt.

SCENE 3

Enter Cinna the poet, and after him the plebeians.

Cinna. I dreamt tonight that I did feast with
Caesar,
And things unluckily charge my fantasy.
I have no will to wander forth of doors,
Yet something leads me forth.
1. Plebeian. What is your name?   5
2. Plebeian. Whither are you going?

270 **forms** literally, long benches, but the sense of social customs and laws is involved here. 277 **upon a wish** immediately as I wished for him. 281–2 **notice . . . them** found out how I had swayed the people. 1 **tonight** last night. 2 **unluckily . . . fantasy** weigh heavily upon my imagination.

3. Plebeian. Where do you dwell?

4. Plebeian. Are you a married man, or a bachelor?

2. Plebeian. Answer every man directly.

1. Plebeian. Ay, and briefly.   10

4. Plebeian. Ay, and wisely.

3. Plebeian. Ay, and truly, you were best.

Cinna. What is my name? Whither am I going?
Where do I dwell? Am I a married man, or a
bachelor? Then, to answer every man directly and
briefly, wisely and truly: wisely I say, I am a
bachelor.   17

2. Plebeian. That's as much as to say, they are fools
that marry; you'll bear me a bang for that, I fear.
Proceed directly.   20

Cinna. Directly, I am going to Caesar's funeral.

1. Plebeian. As a friend or an enemy?

Cinna. As a friend.

2. Plebeian. That matter is answered directly.

4. Plebeian. For your dwelling, briefly.   25

Cinna. Briefly, I dwell by the Capitol.

3. Plebeian. Your name, sir, truly.

Cinna. Truly, my name is Cinna.   28

2. Plebeian. Tear him to pieces, he's a conspirator.

Cinna. I am Cinna the poet, I am Cinna the poet!

4. Plebeian. Tear him for his bad verses, tear him
for his bad verses!

Cinna. I am not Cinna the conspirator.

4. Plebeian. It is no matter, his name's Cinna; pluck
but his name out of his heart, and turn him going.

3. Plebeian. Tear him, tear him; come, brands, ho,
firebrands! To Brutus', to Cassius', burn all. Some to
Decius' house, and some to Casca's, some to
Ligarius'. Away! Go!   *Exeunt all the plebeians.*

9 directly to the point. **19 bear me a bang** get a blow from me.

Act IV

SCENE 1

Enter Antony, Octavius, and Lepidus

Antony. These many then shall die; their names are
  prick'd.
Octavius. Your brother too must die; consent you,
  Lepidus?
Lepidus. I do consent.
Octavius. Prick him down, Antony.   4
Lepidus. Upon condition Publius shall not live,
Who is your sister's son, Mark Antony.
Antony. He shall not live; look, with a spot I damn
  him.
But, Lepidus, go you to Caesar's house,
Fetch the will hither, and we shall determine
How to cut off some charge in legacies.   10
Lepidus. What, shall I find you here?
Octavius. Or here or at the Capitol.   *Exit Lepidus.*
Antony. This is a slight unmeritable man,
Meet to be sent on errands; is it fit,
The three-fold world divided, he should stand   15
One of the three to share it?
Octavius.   So you thought him,

1 prick'd marked. 7 with . . . him with a mark I condemn him.
10 cut off some charge reduce the expense of the legacies.
13 slight unmeritable insignificant and undeserving. 14 Meet fit.
15 three-fold world the Roman empire: Europe, Asia, and Africa.

And took his voice who should be prick'd to die
In our black sentence and proscription.
  Antony. Octavius, I have seen more days than you,
And though we lay these honors on this man,   20
To ease ourselves of divers sland'rous loads,
He shall but bear them as the ass bears gold,
To groan and sweat under the business,
Either led or driven, as we point the way;
And having brought our treasure where we will,   25
Then take we down his load, and turn him off,
Like to the empty ass, to shake his ears,
And graze in commons.
  Octavius.   You may do your will,
But he's a tried and valiant soldier.
  Antony. So is my horse, Octavius, and for that   30
I do appoint him store of provender.
It is a creature that I teach to fight,
To wind, to stop, to run directly on,
His corporal motion govern'd by my spirit.
And, in some taste, is Lepidus but so: 35
He must be taught, and train'd, and bid go forth;
A barren-spirited fellow; one that feeds
On objects, arts, and imitations
Which, out of use and stal'd by other men,
Begin his fashion. Do not talk of him   40
But as a property. And now, Octavius,

18 **proscription** (four syllables) condemnation to exile or death.
21 **ease . . . loads** relieve us of some of the attacks on us for our
actions. 23 **business** three syllables here. 28 **commons** public
pasture. 29 **soldier** three syllables here. 31 **appoint** assign. 33 **wind**
turn. 35 **taste** measure. 37 **spirited** dissyllabic, 'sprited.' 38 **On
. . . imitations** N. 39 **stal'd** soiled, worn out. 40 **Begin his
fashion** are for him the height of fashion. 41 **property** a belonging,
an instrument.

Listen great things. Brutus and Cassius
Are levying powers; we must straight make head;
Therefore let our alliance be combin'd,
Our best friends made, our means stretch'd,   4
And let us presently go sit in council,
How covert matters may be best disclos'd,
And open perils surest answered.
   Octavius. Let us do so, for we are at the stake,
And bayed about with many enemies,   5
And some that smile have in their hearts, I fear,
Millions of mischiefs.   *Exeunt*

SCENE 2

*Drum. Enter Brutus, Lucilius, and the army.
Titinius and Pindarus meet them.*

Brutus. Stand ho!
Lucilius. Give the word ho! and stand.
Brutus. What now, Lucilius, is Cassius near?
Lucilius. He is at hand, and Pindarus is come
To do you salutation from his master.   5
Brutus. He greets me well. Your master, Pindarus
In his own change, or by ill officers,
Hath given me some worthy cause to wish
Things done, undone; but if he be at hand,

43 **make head** raise an army. 45 **made** made certain. **stretch'd**
strained to the utmost. 46 **presently** immediately. 47 **covert
matters** hidden dangers. 49–50 **stake . . . enemies** N. SD **Enter
Brutus** N. 1 **stand** halt. 2 **Give . . . stand** Lucilius passes along
Brutus' command to the troops. 7 **change** change of attitude
toward Brutus. **by ill officers** by the misconduct of subordinates

I shall be satisfied.

Pindarus.   I do not doubt   10
But that my noble master will appear
Such as he is, full of regard and honor.

Brutus. He is not doubted. A word, Lucilius;
How he receiv'd you, let me be resolv'd.   14

Lucilius. With courtesy and with respect enough,
But not with such familiar instances,
Nor with such free and friendly conference,
As he hath us'd of old.

Brutus.   Thou hast describ'd
A hot friend, cooling. Ever note, Lucilius,
When love begins to sicken and decay   20
It useth an enforced ceremony.
There are no tricks in plain and simple faith;
But hollow men, like horses hot at hand,
Make gallant show and promise of their mettle,
                              Low march within.
But when they should endure the bloody spur,   25
They fall their crests, and like deceitful jades
Sink in the trial. Comes his army on?

Lucilius. They mean this night in Sardis to be
        quarter'd;
The greater part, the horse in general,
Are come with Cassius.

Enter Cassius and his Powers.

10 **satisfied** given an explanation. 12 **full . . . honor** worthy of
honorable regard. 16 **familiar instances** tokens of friendship.
17 **conference** conversation. 21 **enforced ceremony** strained
formal manners. 23 **hollow** insincere. **hot at hand** fiery at the
start. 26 **fall their crests** lower their arched necks. **jades** nags.
27 **Sink . . . trial** fail in the test. 29 **horse in general** all the
cavalry.

Brutus.   Hark! he is arriv'd.   30
March gently on to meet him.
    Cassius. Stand ho!
    Brutus. Stand ho! Speak the word along.
    [*1. Officer.*] Stand!
    [*2. Officer.*] Stand!   35
    [*3. Officer.*] Stand!
    Cassius. Most noble brother, you have done me
        wrong.
    Brutus. Judge me, you gods! Wrong I mine
        enemies?
And if not so, how should I wrong a brother?
    Cassius. Brutus, this sober form of yours hides
        wrongs,   40
And when you do them—
    Brutus. Cassius, be content,
Speak your griefs softly, I do know you well.
Before the eyes of both our armies here,
Which should perceive nothing but love from us,   45
Let us not wrangle. Bid them move away;
Then in my tent, Cassius, enlarge your griefs,
And I will give you audience.
    Cassius.   Pindarus,
Bid our commanders lead their charges off
A little from this ground.   50
    Brutus. Lucilius, do you the like, and let no man
Come to our tent till we have done our conference.
Let Lucius and Titinius guard our door.
            Exeunt. Manent Brutus and Cassius.

34 [**1. Officer**] no speech ascriptions are given in the Folio for
these commands. 40 **sober form** calm and grave bearing. 42 **be
content** be calm. 43 **griefs** grievances. **softly** gently. 47 **enlarge
your griefs** explain your grievances in full. 49 **charges** troops.
SD **Manent Brutus and Cassius** N.

Cassius. That you have wrong'd me doth appear in
    this:
You have condemn'd and noted Lucius Pella   55
For taking bribes here of the Sardians;
Wherein my letters, praying on his side,
Because I knew the man, was slighted off.
  Brutus. You wrong'd yourself to write in such a
    case.
  Cassius. In such a time as this, it is not meet   60
That every nice offense should bear his comment.
  Brutus. Let me tell you, Cassius, you yourself
Are much condemn'd to have an itching palm,
To sell and mart your offices for gold
To undeservers.
  Cassius.   I an itching palm!   65
You know that you are Brutus that speaks this,
Or, by the gods, this speech were else your last.
  Brutus. The name of Cassius honors this corrup-
    tion,
And chastisement doth therefore hide his head.
  Cassius. Chastisement!   70
  Brutus. Remember March, the ides of March re-
    member:
Did not great Julius bleed for justice' sake?
What villain touch'd his body, that did stab,
And not for justice? What, shall one of us,
That struck the foremost man of all this world   75

55 noted marked. 57 **praying . . . side** interceding for him. 58
slighted off tossed slightingly aside. 61 **nice** trivial. **bear his
comment** be criticized. **his** its. 63 **condemn'd to have** blamed for
having. 64 **mart your offices** market your positions. 68 **honors
. . . corruption** makes these corrupt practices appear honest.
73–4 **What . . . justice** what man who stabbed Caesar was such
a villain that he did not do so for justice' sake?

                              75

But for supporting robbers, shall we now
Contaminate our fingers with base bribes,
And sell the mighty space of our large honors
For so much trash as may be grasped thus?
I had rather be a dog and bay the moon,   80
Than such a Roman.
    Cassius.   Brutus, bait not me,
I'll not endure it; you forget yourself
To hedge me in. I am a soldier, I,
Older in practice, abler than yourself
To make conditions.   85
  Brutus. Go to; you are not, Cassius.
  Cassius. I am.
  Brutus. I say you are not.
  Cassius. Urge me no more, I shall forget myself.
Have mind upon your health, tempt me no further.
  Brutus. Away, slight man!   91
  Cassius. Is't possible?
  Brutus. Hear me, for I will speak.
Must I give way and room to your rash choler?
Shall I be frighted when a madman stares?   95
  Cassius. O ye gods, ye gods! Must I endure all this?
  Brutus. All this? ay, more: fret till your proud
      heart break.
Go show your slaves how choleric you are,
And make your bondmen tremble. Must I budge?
Must I observe you? Must I stand and crouch   100
Under your testy humor? By the gods,

76 **supporting robbers** N. **78–9 And sell . . . grasped thus** N.
80 **bay** bark at. 81 **bait** harass. 83 **hedge me in** control me.
85 **make conditions** manage affairs. 89 **Urge** push. 91 **slight man**
worthless fellow. 94 **give . . . choler** allow your reckless anger
free play. 95 **stares** glares. 100 **observe** be humbly reverent to.
101 **testy humor** irritability.
   76

You shall digest the venom of your spleen,
Though it do split you. For, from this day forth,
I'll use you for my mirth, yea, for my laughter,
When you are waspish.   105
  Cassius. Is it come to this?
  Brutus. You say you are a better soldier;
Let it appear so; make your vaunting true,
And it shall please me well. For mine own part,
I shall be glad to learn of noble men.   110
  Cassius. You wrong me every way;
You wrong me Brutus.
I said, an elder soldier, not a better.
Did I say 'better'?
  Brutus. If you did, I care not.   115
  Cassius. When Caesar liv'd, he durst not thus have
    mov'd me.
  Brutus. Peace, peace, you durst not so have
    tempted him.
  Cassius. I durst not?
  Brutus. No.
  Cassius. What? durst not tempt him?   120
  Brutus. For your life you durst not.
  Cassius. Do not presume too much upon my love;
I may do that I shall be sorry for.
  Brutus. You have done that you should be sorry
    for.
There is no terror, Cassius, in your threats,   125
For I am arm'd so strong in honesty
That they pass by me as the idle wind,
Which I respect not. I did send to you
For certain sums of gold, which you denied me,

102 **spleen** the source of sudden passions N. 110 **learn of** learn
from. 116 **mov'd** stirred. 117 **tempted** provoked. 126 **honesty**
integrity.

For I can raise no money by vile means;   130
By heaven, I had rather coin my heart,
And drop my blood for drachmas, than to wring
From the hard hands of peasants their vile trash
By any indirection. I did send
To you for gold to pay my legions,   135
Which you denied me. Was that done like Cassius?
Should I have answer'd Caius Cassius so?
When Marcus Brutus grows so covetous,
To lock such rascal counters from his friends,
Be ready, gods, with all your thunderbolts;   140
Dash him to pieces!
  Cassius. I denied you not.
  Brutus. You did.
  Cassius. I did not. He was but a fool
That brought my answer back. Brutus hath riv'd my
    heart: 145
A friend should bear his friend's infirmities,
But Brutus makes mine greater than they are.
  Brutus. I do not, till you practice them on me.
  Cassius. You love me not.
  Brutus. I do not like your faults.   150
  Cassius. A friendly eye could never see such faults.
  Brutus. A flatterer's would not, though they do
    appear
As huge as high Olympus.
  Cassius. Come, Antony, and young Octavius, come,
Revenge yourselves alone on Cassius,   155
For Cassius is aweary of the world:
Hated by one he loves; brav'd by his brother;
Check'd like a bondman; all his faults observ'd,

---

134 **indirection** dishonesty. 135 **legions** three syllables here.
139 **rascal counters** worthless coins. 145 **riv'd** split. 146 **infirmities**
weaknesses. 157 **brav'd** taunted. 158 **Check'd** scolded.

Set in a notebook, learn'd, and conn'd by rote,
To cast into my teeth. O, I could weep   160
My spirit from mine eyes. There is my dagger,
And here my naked breast; within, a heart
Dearer than Pluto's mine, richer than gold;
If that thou be'st a Roman, take it forth.
I that denied thee gold, will give my heart.   165
Strike as thou didst at Caesar, for I know
When thou didst hate him worst, thou lov'dst him
      better
Than ever thou lov'dst Cassius.
    Brutus. Sheathe your dagger;
Be angry when you will, it shall have scope.   170
Do what you will, dishonor shall be humor.
O Cassius, you are yoked with a lamb
That carries anger as the flint bears fire,
Who, much enforced, shows a hasty spark,
And straight is cold again.   175
    Cassius. Hath Cassius liv'd
To be but mirth and laughter to his Brutus,
When grief and blood ill-temper'd vexeth him?
    Brutus. When I spoke that I was ill-temper'd too.
    Cassius. Do you confess so much? Give me your
      hand.   180
    Brutus. And my heart too.
    Cassius. O Brutus!
    Brutus. What's the matter?
    Cassius. Have not you love enough to bear with me,
When that rash humor which my mother gave me

159 Set . . . rote written down, studied, and memorized. 160
cast into my teeth throw into my face. 163 Dearer worth more.
Pluto's mine the riches of the underworld. 170 scope freedom.
171 humor mere caprices. 178 blood ill-temper'd disordered condition. 185 rash humor excitable temperament.

Makes me forgetful? 186

Brutus. Yes, Cassius, and from henceforth
When you are overearnest with your Brutus,
He'll think your mother chides, and leave you so.

Enter a Poet.

Poet. Let me go in to see the generals; 190
There is some grudge between 'em, 'tis not meet
They be alone.

Lucilius. You shall not come to them.

Poet. Nothing but death shall stay me.

Cassius. How now? What's the matter? 195

Poet. For shame, you generals, what do you mean?
Love, and be friends, as two such men should be,
For I have seen more years, I'm sure, than ye.

Cassius. Ha, ha! how vildely doth this cynic rhyme!

Brutus. Get you hence, sirrah; saucy fellow, hence!

Cassius. Bear with him, Brutus, 'tis his fashion.

Brutus. I'll know his humor, when he knows his
time.
What should the wars do with these jigging fools?
Companion, hence! 204

Cassius. Away, away, be gone! *Exit Poet.*

Brutus. Lucilius and Titinius, bid the commanders
Prepare to lodge their companies tonight.

Cassius. And come yourselves, and bring Messala
with you
Immediately to us.

Brutus. Lucius, a bowl of wine! 210

Cassius. I did not think you could have been so
angry.

189 **leave you so** let it go at that. SD **Enter a Poet** N. 199 **vildely**
vilely. 202 **I'll know . . . time** I will accept his peculiarity when
he knows the proper time for it. 204 **Companion** base fellow.

Brutus. O Cassius, I am sick of many griefs.

Cassius. Of your philosophy you make no use,
If you give place to accidental evils.   214

Brutus. No man bears sorrow better. Portia is dead.

Cassius. Ha? Portia?

Brutus. She is dead.

Cassius. How scap'd I killing when I cross'd you so?
O insupportable and touching loss!
Upon what sickness?   220

Brutus. Impatient of my absence,
And grief that young Octavius with Mark Antony
Have made themselves so strong—for with her death
That tidings came—with this she fell distract,
And, her attendants absent, swallow'd fire.   225

Cassius. And died so?

Brutus. Even so.

Cassius. O ye immortal gods!

Enter Boy with wine and tapers.

Brutus. Speak no more of her. Give me a bowl of
    wine.   229
In this I bury all unkindness, Cassius.   *Drinks.*

Cassius. My heart is thirsty for that noble pledge.
Fill, Lucius, till the wine o'erswell the cup;
I cannot drink too much of Brutus' love.

Enter Titinius and Messala.

Brutus. Come in, Titinius. Welcome, good Messala.
Now sit we close about this taper here,   235

213 **philosophy** Brutus is a Stoic. 214 **accidental evils** evils that
come about by chance. 219 **touching** that which touches the very
heart, grievous. 221 **Impatient** unable to endure. 224 **with this**
at this time. **fell distract** became distracted.

And call in question our necessities.

Cassius. Portia, art thou gone?

Brutus. No more, I pray you.
Messala, I have here received letters,
That young Octavius and Mark Antony   240
Come down upon us with a mighty power,
Bending their expedition toward Philippi.

Messala. Myself have letters of the selfsame tenor.

Brutus. With what addition?

Messala. That by proscription and bills of out-
      lawry,   245
Octavius, Antony, and Lepidus,
Have put to death an hundred senators.

Brutus. Therein our letters do not well agree;
Mine speak of seventy senators that died
By their proscriptions, Cicero being one.   250

Cassius. Cicero one?

Messala. Cicero is dead, and by that order of pro-
      scription.
Had you your letters from your wife, my lord?

Brutus. No, Messala.   254

Messala. Nor nothing in your letters writ of her?

Brutus. Nothing, Messala.

Messala. That, methinks, is strange.

Brutus. Why ask you? Hear you aught of her in
      yours?

Messala. No, my lord.   259

Brutus. Now, as you are a Roman, tell me true.

Messala. Then like a Roman bear the truth I tell,
For certain she is dead, and by strange manner.

236 call . . . necessities discuss our needful courses. 242 Bending
. . . expedition directing their quick march. 243 tenor purport.
253ff. Had you your letters . . . N.

Brutus. Why, farewell, Portia. We must die, Messala.
With meditating that she must die once,
I have the patience to endure it now.   265
  Messala. Even so great men great losses should
    endure.
  Cassius. I have as much of this in art as you,
But yet my nature could not bear it so.
  Brutus. Well, to our work alive. What do you think
Of marching to Philippi presently?   270
  Cassius. I do not think it good.
  Brutus. Your reason?
  Cassius. This it is:
'Tis better that the enemy seek us;
So shall he waste his means, weary his soldiers,   275
Doing himself offense, whilst we, lying still,
Are full of rest, defense, and nimbleness.
  Brutus. Good reasons must of force give place to
    better.
The people 'twixt Philippi and this ground
Do stand but in a forc'd affection,   280
For they have grudg'd us contribution.
The enemy, marching along by them,
By them shall make a fuller number up,
Come on refresh'd, new-added, and encourag'd;
From which advantage shall we cut him off,   285
If at Philippi we do face him there,
These people at our back.
  Cassius. Hear me, good brother.

264 once some day. 267 I have . . . you I am as skilled in con-
trolling myself as you are. 269 alive which concerns the living.
270 presently immediately. 278 of force of necessity. 280 forc'd
affection compulsory friendship. 281 grudg'd us contribution
(five syllables) begrudged us aid.

                                                          83

Brutus. Under your pardon. You must note beside,
That we have tried the utmost of our friends,   290
Our legions are brimful, our cause is ripe;
The enemy increaseth every day,
We, at the height, are ready to decline.
There is a tide in the affairs of men,
Which taken at the flood, leads on to fortune;   295
Omitted, all the voyage of their life
Is bound in shallows and in miseries.
On such a full sea are we now afloat,
And we must take the current when it serves,
Or lose our ventures.   300
Cassius. Then, with your will, go on: we'll along
Ourselves, and meet them at Philippi.
Brutus. The deep of night is crept upon our talk,
And nature must obey necessity,
Which we will niggard with a little rest.   305
There is no more to say.
Cassius. No more. Good night:
Early tomorrow will we rise, and hence.

Enter Lucius.

Brutus. Lucius, my gown. Farewell, good Messala,
Good night, Titinius. Noble, noble Cassius,   310
Good night, and good repose.
Cassius.   O my dear brother,
This was an ill beginning of the night.
Never come such division 'tween our souls;
Let it not, Brutus.

289 **Under your pardon** begging your pardon. 290 **tried . . .
friends** used our allies as much as possible. 296 **Omitted** if it is
neglected. 300 **ventures** goods which have been risked on an
enterprise. 301 **with your will** as you desire. 305 **niggard** scant.
309 **gown** robe.

Enter Lucius with the gown.

Brutus. Everything is well.   315
Cassius. Good night, my lord.
Brutus. Good night, good brother.
Titinius, Messala. Good night, Lord Brutus.
Brutus. Farewell, every one.   *Exeunt.*
Give me the gown. Where is thy instrument?   320
Lucius. Here in the tent.
Brutus. What, thou speak'st drowsily?
Poor knave, I blame thee not, thou art o'erwatch'd.
Call Claudio and some other of my men;
I'll have them sleep on cushions in my tent.   325
Lucius. Varrus and Claudio!

Enter Varrus and Claudio.

Varrus. Calls my lord?
Brutus. I pray you, sirs, lie in my tent and sleep;
It may be I shall raise you by and by
On business to my brother Cassius.   330
Varrus. So please you, we will stand and watch your
    pleasure.
Brutus. I will not have it so; lie down, good sirs;
It may be I shall otherwise bethink me.
Look, Lucius, here's the book I sought for so;
I put it in the pocket of my gown.   335
Lucius. I was sure your lordship did not give it me.
Brutus. Bear with me, good boy, I am much forget-
    ful.
Canst thou hold up thy heavy eyes awhile,
And touch thy instrument a strain or two?

323 **knave** boy. **o'erwatch'd** worn out from being too long on
watch. 329 **raise** rouse. 331 **watch** wakefully await. 333 **otherwise . . . me** change my mind. 339 **touch . . . two** play a tune
or two on your lute.

85

Lucius. Ay, my lord, an't please you.   340
Brutus. It does, my boy.
I trouble thee too much, but thou art willing.
Lucius. It is my duty, sir.
Brutus. I should not urge thy duty past thy might;
I know young bloods look for a time of rest.   345
Lucius. I have slept, my lord, already.
Brutus. It was well done, and thou shalt sleep again.
I will not hold thee long. If I do live,
I will be good to thee.   *Music, and a song.*
This is a sleepy tune. O murd'rous slumber,   350
Layest thou thy leaden mace upon my boy,
That plays thee music? Gentle knave, good night;
I will not do thee so much wrong to wake thee.
If thou dost nod, thou break'st thy instrument;   354
I'll take it from thee, and, good boy, good night.
Let me see, let me see, is not the leaf turn'd down
Where I left reading? Here it is, I think,

Enter the Ghost of Caesar.

How ill this taper burns. Ha! Who comes here?
I think it is the weakness of mine eyes
That shapes this monstrous apparition.   360
It comes upon me. Art thou any thing?
Art thou some god, some angel, or some divell,
That mak'st my blood cold and my hair to stare?
Speak to me what thou art.
Ghost. Thy evil spirit, Brutus.   365
Brutus. Why com'st thou?
Ghost. To tell thee thou shalt see me at Philippi.

344 urge enforce. 350 murd'rous because sleep makes the sleeper
appear lifeless. 351 leaden mace N. 358 ill . . . burns accepted
sign of a spirit's presence. 360 shapes gives form to. 363 stare
stand on end.

Brutus. Well, then I shall see thee again!

Ghost. Ay, at Philippi.

Brutus. Why, I will see thee at Philippi then. 370
Now I have taken heart, thou vanishest.
Ill spirit, I would hold more talk with thee.
Boy, Lucius, Varrus, Claudio, sirs; awake;
Claudio!

Lucius. The strings, my lord, are false. 375

Brutus. He thinks he still is at his instrument.
Lucius, awake!

Lucius. My lord!

Brutus. Didst thou dream, Lucius, that thou so
      criedst out?

Lucius. My lord, I do not know that I did cry. 380

Brutus. Yes, that thou did'st. Did'st thou see any-
      thing?

Lucius. Nothing, my lord.

Brutus. Sleep again, Lucius. Sirrah, Claudio, fellow,
Thou; awake!

Varrus. My lord? 385

Claudio. My lord?

Brutus. Why did you so cry out, sirs, in your
      sleep?

Both. Did we, my lord?

Brutus. Ay; saw you anything?

Varrus. No, my lord, I saw nothing. 390

Claudio. Nor I, my lord.

Brutus. Go, and commend me to my brother Cassius.
Bid him set on his powers betimes before,
And we will follow.

Both. It shall be done, my lord.   *Exeunt.*

375 false out of tune. 393 betimes early.

Act V

Enter Octavius, Antony, and their army.

Octavius. Now, Antony, our hopes are answered.
You said the enemy would not come down,
But keep the hills and upper regions.
It proves not so; their battles are at hand,
They mean to warn us at Philippi here,   5
Answering before we do demand of them.

   Antony. Tut, I am in their bosoms, and I know
Wherefore they do it. They could be content
To visit other places, and come down
With fearful bravery, thinking by this face   10
To fasten in our thoughts that they have courage;
But 'tis not so.

Enter a Messenger.

Messenger. Prepare you, generals,
The enemy comes on in gallant show,
Their bloody sign of battle is hung out,   15
And something to be done immediately.

3 regions three syllables here. **4 battles** armies. **5 warn** challenge.
6 demand of them bring them to battle. **7 in their bosoms** know
their secrets. **8–9 They . . . places** they would be happy to be
elsewhere. **10 fearful bravery** brave show which masks fear. **face**
pretense. **15 bloody sign** red flag signaling immediate combat.

Antony. Octavius, lead your battle softly on
Upon the left hand of the even field.
  Octavius. Upon the right hand I; keep thou the left.
  Antony. Why do you cross me in this exigent?   20
  Octavius. I do not cross you; but I will do so.

March.

Drum. Enter Brutus, Cassius, and their army.

Brutus. They stand and would have parley.
  Cassius. Stand fast, Titinius, we must out and talk.
  Octavius. Mark Antony, shall we give sign of
      battle?   24
  Antony. No, Caesar, we will answer on their charge.
Make forth; the generals would have some words.
  Octavius. Stir not until the signal.
  Brutus. Words before blows: is it so, countrymen?
  Octavius. Not that we love words better, as you do.
  Brutus. Good words are better than bad strokes,
      Octavius.   30
  Antony. In your bad strokes, Brutus, you give good
      words;
Witness the hole you made in Caesar's heart,
Crying 'Long live, Hail, Caesar!'
  Cassius.   Antony,
The posture of your blows are yet unknown;
But for your words, they rob the Hybla bees,   35
And leave them honeyless.
  Antony. Not stingless too!

17 softly slowly. 18 even flat. 20 **exigent** crisis. 21 **I do . . . so**
I am not merely thwarting you, but I shall do as I desire. 25
answer . . . charge fight when they attack. 26 **Make forth** step
forward. 27 **Stir . . . signal** presumably addressed to his own
commanders. 34 **posture** nature. 35 **Hybla** town in Sicily famous
for its honey.

Brutus. O yes, and soundless too,
For you have stolne their buzzing, Antony,
And very wisely threat before you sting.   40
   Antony. Villains! you did not so when your vile
      daggers
Hack'd one another in the sides of Caesar;
You show'd your teeth like apes, and fawn'd like
      hounds,
And bow'd like bondmen, kissing Caesar's feet;
Whilst damned Casca, like a cur, behind   45
Strooke Caesar on the neck. O you flatterers.
   Cassius. Flatterers? Now, Brutus, thank yourself:
This tongue had not offended so today.
If Cassius might have rul'd.
   Octavius. Come, come, the cause. If arguing makes
      us sweat,   50
The proof of it will turn to redder drops.
Look, I draw a sword against conspirators;
When think you that the sword goes up again?
Never, till Caesar's three and thirty wounds
Be well aveng'd; or till another Caesar   55
Have added slaughter to the sword of traitors.
   Brutus. Caesar, thou canst not die by traitors'
      hands,
Unless thou bring'st them with thee.
   Octavius.   So I hope.
I was not born to die on Brutus' sword.   59
   Brutus. O, if thou wert the noblest of thy strain,
Young man, thou couldst not die more honorable.

---

39 **stolne** stolen. 43 **show'd your teeth** grinned. 46 **Strooke** struck. 48–9 **This tongue . . . rul'd** Cassius refers to his own plan to kill Antony with Caesar. 50 **cause** matter at hand. 51 **proof of it** test of our quarrel. 53 **goes up** will be sheathed. 60 **strain** family.

Cassius. A peevish schoolboy, worthless of such honor,
Join'd with a masker and a reveler.
Antony. Old Cassius still.
Octavius. Come, Antony, away!   65
Defiance, traitors, hurl we in your teeth.
If you dare fight today, come to the field;
If not, when you have stomachs.
                    Exeunt Octavius, Antony, and army.
Cassius. Why now, blow wind, swell billow, and swim bark.
The storm is up, and all is on the hazard.   70
Brutus. Ho, Lucilius, hark, a word with you.
                    Lucilius and Messala stand forth.
Lucilius. My lord?
Cassius. Messala.
Messala. What says my general?
Cassius. Messala, this is my birthday; as this very day   75
Was Cassius born. Give me thy hand, Messala;
Be thou my witness that against my will,
As Pompey was, am I compell'd to set
Upon one battle all our liberties.
You know that I held Epicurus strong,   80
And his opinion; now I change my mind,
And partly credit things that do presage.
Coming from Sardis, on our former ensign

62 peevish childish. worthless unworthy. such honor i.e. dying on Brutus' sword. 63 masker see I.2.204-5 N. 68 stomachs courage. 70 on the hazard risked on the outcome, a dicer's term. 78 Pompey at the battle of Pharsalia where he was defeated by Julius Caesar in 48 B.C., Pompey fought against his better judgment. set stake. 80 held Epicurus strong N. 82 presage fortell the future. 83 former foremost.

91

Two mighty eagles fell, and there they perch'd,
Gorging and feeding from our soldiers' hands,   85
Who to Philippi here consorted us.
This morning are they fled away and gone,
And in their steeds do ravens, crows, and kites
Fly o'er our heads, and downward look on us,
As we were sickly prey; their shadows seem   90
A canopy most fatal, under which
Our army lies, ready to give up the ghost.
  Messala. Believe not so.
  Cassius. I but believe it partly,
For I am fresh of spirit and resolv'd   95
To meet all perils very constantly.
  Brutus. Even so, Lucilius.
  Cassius. Now, most noble Brutus,
The gods today stand friendly, that we may,
Lovers in peace, lead on our days to age.   100
But since the affairs of men rest still uncertain,
Let's reason with the worst that may befall.
If we do lose this battle, then is this
The very last time we shall speak together.
What are you, then, determined to do?   105
  Brutus. Even by the rule of that philosophy
By which I did blame Cato for the death
Which he did give himself—I know not how,
But I do find it cowardly and vile,

88 **steeds** steads, places. 91 **fatal** fateful. 96 **constantly** firmly.
97 **Even so, Lucilius** this is the end of Brutus' whispered conversation with Lucilius. 99 **The gods** may the gods. 100 **Lovers**
friends. 101 **the affairs** read 'th' affairs.' **still incertain** always
uncertain. 102 **reason with** consider. 106 **that philosophy** Stoicism;
the Stoics rejected suicide as a cowardly answer to life's ills.
107 **Cato** Cato of Utica killed himself in 46 B.C.

For fear of what might fall, so to prevent   110
The time of life—arming myself with patience,
To stay the providence of some high powers
That govern us below.
  Cassius. Then, if we lose this battle,
You are contented to be led in triumph   115
Thorow the streets of Rome?
  Brutus. No, Cassius, no; think not, thou noble
      Roman,
That ever Brutus will go bound to Rome;
He bears too great a mind. But this same day
Must end that work the ides of March begun.   120
And whether we shall meet again, I know not.
Therefore our everlasting farewell take:
Forever, and forever, farewell, Cassius.
If we do meet again, why, we shall smile;
If not, why then this parting was well made.   125
  Cassius. Forever, and forever, farewell, Brutus.
If we do meet again, we'll smile indeed;
If not, 'tis true, this parting was well made.
  Brutus. Why then, lead on. O, that a man might
      know
The end of this day's business, ere it come;   130
But it sufficeth that the day will end,
And then the end is known. Come, ho! away!
                    Exeunt.

110–11 **prevent The time** bring about the end before its natural occurrence. 112 **stay** await.

SCENE 2

Alarum. Enter Brutus and Messala.

Brutus. Ride, ride, Messala, ride and give these bills
Unto the legions on the other side.   *Loud alarum.*
Let them set on at once, for I perceive
But cold demeanor in Octavius' wing,
And sudden push gives them the overthrow.   5
Ride, ride, Messala, let them all come down.

                                        Exeunt.

Alarums. Enter Cassius and Titinius.

Cassius. O look, Titinius, look, the villains fly.
Myself have to mine own turn'd enemy:
This ensign here of mine was turning back;
I slew the coward, and did take it from him.   10
    Titinius. O Cassius, Brutus gave the word too early,
Who, having some advantage on Octavius,
Took it too eagerly; his soldiers fell to spoil,
Whilst we by Antony are all enclos'd.   14

Enter Pindarus.

Pindarus. Fly further off, my lord, fly further off;
Mark Antony is in your tents, my lord.
Fly, therefore, noble Cassius, fly far off.

1 **bills** written orders. 2 **other side** the wing commanded by
Cassius. 4 **cold demeanor** lack of battle fire. SD **Alarums** N.
7 **the villains** his own troops. 9 **ensign** the standard bearer.
10 **it** the standard. 13 **fell to spoil** began looting.

Cassius. This hill is far enough. Look, look,
    Titinius;
Are those my tents where I perceive the fire?
 Titinius. They are, my lord.   20
 Cassius. Titinius, if thou lovest me,
Mount thou my horse, and hide thy spurs in him,
Till he have brought thee up to yonder troops
And here again, that I may rest assur'd
Whether yond troops are friend or enemy.   25
 Titinius. I will be here again, even with a thought.
                        Exit.

 Cassius. Go, Pindarus, get higher on that hill;
My sight was ever thick; regard Titinius,
And tell me what thou not'st about the field.
This day I breathed first, time is come round,   30
And where I did begin, there shall I end;
My life is run his compass. Sirrah, what news?
 Pindarus. (*Above.*) O my lord!
 Cassius. What news?
 Pindarus. Titinius is enclosed round about   35
With horsemen that make to him on the spur,
Yet he spurs on. Now they are almost on him;
Now, Titinius! Now some light; O, he lights too.
He's tane.   *Shout.*
        And hark, they shout for joy.
 Cassius. Come down, behold no more.   40
O, coward that I am, to live so long,
To see my best friend tane before my face.

        Enter Pindarus.

26 **even with** quick as. 28 **thick** dim. **regard** look about. 32 **his compass** its circle. 33 **Above** Pindarus has gone up to the upper gallery of the stage while Cassius remains below on the main stage. 38 **light** dismount. 39 **tane** syncopated form of 'taken.'

Come hither, sirrah.
In Parthia did I take thee prisoner,
And then I swore thee, saving of thy life,   45
That whatsoever I did bid thee do,
Thou shouldst attempt it. Come now, keep thine
    oath;
Now be a freeman, and with this good sword,
That ran through Caesar's bowels, search this
    bosom.
Stand not to answer; here, take thou the hilts,   50
And when my face is cover'd, as 'tis now,
Guide thou the sword—Caesar, thou art reveng'd,
Even with the sword that kill'd thee.
    Pindarus. So, I am free, yet would not so have
    been,
Durst I have done my will. O Cassius,   55
Far from this country Pindarus shall run,
Where never Roman shall take note of him.

Enter Titinius and Messala.

    Messala. It is but change, Titinius; for Octavius
Is overthrown by noble Brutus' power,
As Cassius' legions are by Antony.   60
    Titinius. These tidings will well comfort Cassius.
    Messala. Where did you leave him?
    Titinius.   All disconsolate,
With Pindarus his bondman, on this hill.
    Messala. Is not that he that lies upon the ground?
    Titinius. He lies not like the living. O my heart!
    Messala. Is not that he?

---

45 **swore thee** made thee swear. **saving of** when I saved. 48 **free-man** he will be freed from slavery on Cassius' death. 49 **search** probe. 58 **change** exchange.

We shall try fortune in a second fight.　　　*Exeunt.*

Alarum. Enter Brutus, Messala, Cato, Lucilius,
and Flavius.

Brutus. Yet, countrymen, O yet hold up your
　　heads!
Cato. What bastard doth not? Who will go with
　　me?　　　　　　　　　　　　　　　　　120
I will proclaim my name about the field.
I am the son of Marcus Cato, ho!
A foe to tyrants, and my country's friend.
I am the son of Marcus Cato, ho!　　　　124

Enter soldiers, and fight.

[*Brutus.*] And I am Brutus, Marcus Brutus, I;
Brutus, my country's friend; know me for Brutus!
Lucilius. O young and noble Cato, art thou down?
Why now thou diest as bravely as Titinius,
And may'st be honor'd, being Cato's son.
1. Soldier. Yield, or thou diest.　　　　　130
Lucilius. Only I yield to die.
There is so much that thou wilt kill me straight.
Kill Brutus, and be honor'd in his death.
1. Soldier. We must not. A noble prisoner.　　134

Enter Antony.

2. Soldier. Room, ho! Tell Antony, Brutus is tane.
1. Soldier. I'll tell the news. Here comes the general.
Brutus is tane, Brutus is tane, my lord.
Antony. Where is he?

125 [Brutus] N. 131 **Only . . . die** I yield only in order to die.
132 **There . . . much** presumably Lucilius offers the soldier
money. 135 **tane** taken.

Lucilius. Safe, Antony; Brutus is safe enough.
I dare assure thee that no enemy   140
Shall ever take alive the noble Brutus.
The gods defend him from so great a shame!
When you do find him, or alive or dead,
He will be found like Brutus, like himself.
  Antony. This is not Brutus, friend, but, I assure
    you,   145
A prize no less in worth. Keep this man safe,
Give him all kindness. I had rather have
Such men my friends than enemies. Go on,
And see where Brutus be alive or dead,
And bring us word, unto Octavius' tent,   150
How everything is chanc'd.   *Exeunt.*

SCENE 3

Enter Brutus, Dardanius, Clitus, Strato,
and Volumnius.

  Brutus. Come, poor remains of friends, rest on this
    rock.
  Clitus. Statilius show'd the torchlight, but, my lord,
He came not back. He is or tane or slain.
  Brutus. Sit thee down, Clitus; 'slaying' is the word;
It is a deed in fashion. Hark thee, Clitus.   5
                                          [*Whispers.*]
  Clitus. What, I, my lord? No, not for all the world.
  Brutus. Peace, then, no words.
  Clitus. I'll rather kill myself.

149 **where** whether. 151 **chanc'd** turned out. 2 **torchlight** Statilius
is a scout who has gone ahead to see if all is well.

Brutus. Hark thee, Dardanius.

Dardanius. Shall I do such a deed? 10

Clitus. O Dardanius!

Dardanius. O Clitus!

Clitus. What ill request did Brutus make to thee?

Dardanius. To kill him, Clitus. Look, he meditates.

Clitus. Now is that noble vessel full of grief, 15
That it runs over even at his eyes.

Brutus. Come hither, good Volumnius, list a word.

Volumnius. What says my lord?

Brutus. Why this, Volumnius:
The ghost of Caesar hath appear'd to me 20
Two several times by night; at Sardis once,
And this last night here in Philippi fields.
I know my hour is come.

Volumnius.   Not so, my lord.

Brutus. Nay, I am sure it is, Volumnius.
Thou seest the world, Volumnius, how it goes, 25
Our enemies have beat us to the pit;   *Low alarums.*
It is more worthy to leap in ourselves,
Than tarry till they push us. Good Volumnius,
Thou know'st that we two went to school together;
Even for that our love of old, I prithee, 30
Hold thou my sword hilts whilst I run on it.

Volumnius. That's not an office for a friend, my
    lord.   *Alarum still.*

Clitus. Fly, fly, my lord, there is no tarrying here.

Brutus. Farewell to you, and you, and you, Volum-
    nius.

Strato, thou hast been all this while asleep; 35
Farewell to thee too, Strato. Countrymen,
My heart doth joy that yet, in all my life

21 **several** separate. 25 **how it goes** how matters are turning out.
26 **pit** trap for wild animals.

I found no man but he was true to me.
I shall have glory by this losing day
More than Octavius and Mark Antony   40
By this vile conquest shall attain unto.
So fare you well at once, for Brutus' tongue
Hath almost ended his life's history;
Night hangs upon mine eyes; my bones would rest,
That have but labor'd to attain this hour.   45
                    Alarum. Cry within, Fly, fly, fly.
  Clitus. Fly, my lord, fly!
  Brutus.   Hence, I will follow.
I prithee, Strato, stay thou by thy lord.
Thou art a fellow of a good respect;
Thy life hath had some smatch of honor in it;
Hold then my sword, and turn away thy face,   50
While I do run upon it. Wilt thou, Strato?
  Strato. Give me your hand first. Fare you well, my
    lord.
  Brutus. Farewell, good Strato—Caesar, now be
    still,
I kill'd not thee with half so good a will.   *Dies.*

            Alarum. Retreat. Enter Antony, Octavius,
                Messala, Lucilius, and the army.

  Octavius. What man is that?   55
  Messala. My master's man. Strato, where is thy
    master?
  Strato. Free from the bondage you are in, Messala;
The conquerors can but make a fire of him;
For Brutus only overcame himself,
And no man else hath honor by his death.   60

---

45 but only, exclusively. 49 smatch flavor. 58 make a fire burn
his body on the funeral pyre. 59 only alone.

Lucilius. So Brutus should be found. I thank thee,
    Brutus,
That thou hast prov'd Lucilius' saying true.
Octavius. All that serv'd Brutus, I will entertain
    them.
Fellow, wilt thou bestow thy time with me?
Strato. Ay, if Messala will prefer me to you.   65
Octavius. Do so, good Messala.
Messala. How died my master, Strato?
Strato. I held the sword, and he did run on it.
Messala. Octavius, then take him to follow thee,
That did the latest service to my master.   70
  Antony. This was the noblest Roman of them all;
All the conspirators save only he
Did that they did in envy of great Caesar;
He, only in a general honest thought
And common good to all, made one of them.   75
His life was gentle, and the elements
So mix'd in him that Nature might stand up
And say to all world, 'This was a man!'
  Octavius. According to his virtue let us use him,
With all respect and rites of burial.   80
Within my tent his bones tonight shall lie,
Most like a soldier, ordered honorably.
So call the field to rest, and let's away
To part the glories of this happy day.
                            Exeunt omnes.

63 **entertain** employ. 65 **prefer** recommend. 70 **latest service** last
duty. 74–5 **He . . . them** Brutus was the only one of the conspirators who acted out of an honorable purpose and a concern
for the good of all. 76 **gentle** noble. **elements** N. 79 **use** treat.
82 **ordered** arrayed, treated with all honor. 84 **part** share.

NOTES

Act I, Scene 1

1SD Marullus The Folio reading is *Murellus*, an incorrect spelling of the name as it appears in Plutarch. (References to the Folio are, throughout, to the First Folio of 1623.)

16 Flavius Editors have traditionally given this speech to Marullus, despite the clear reading of the Folio to the contrary, on the ground that since Marullus has been questioning the Cobbler it is more logical for him to continue. It is not, however, more dramatic, for what we have here is a scene in which the two incensed aristocrats are attacking the impudent mob, and what could be more fitting than for them to alternate in their attack. Besides, where the Folio reading makes sense at all, as it surely does here, I do not see how we are justified in changing it.

19 out . . . mend The Cobbler begins here another series of bad puns which allow him to be insolent while maintaining an appearance of simply answering the questions put to him. Marullus takes the line 'if you be out, sir, I can mend you' in the sense of a threat to correct him of his bad temper, but the Cobbler can escape into the other meaning, 'if your shoes be worn out I can repair them.' Note also the Cobbler's punning on *awl, all, withal* in his next speech.

33 triumph A triumph was a celebration given by the city for a military victor. The occasion for this particular triumph was Caesar's victory over the sons of Pompey at Munda, in Spain, March 17, 45 B.C. Plutarch tells us that the triumph was resented by many Romans because it was the first time that the defeat of one Roman by another had been made a cause for public celebration.

66–7 images . . . ceremonies The *images* are statues of Caesar set up to celebrate his triumph, and the *ceremonies* which Flavius plans to strip from them are the symbols, probably wreaths, with which they have been decorated.

104

69 Lupercal Roman festival of purification held on February 15. Young men called *Luperci* ran around the Palatine hill and by striking those who stood in their way with thongs of goatskin prevented barrenness. These thongs were called *februa* from *februare*, 'to purify,' and thus the month *februarius*. Shakespeare has combined the two events of the Lupercal and Caesar's triumph, which was actually held the preceding October.

Act I, Scene 2

Scene 2 No scene divisions except I.1 are marked in the Folio text, and it is probable that in the Elizabethan theater action was continuous without interruptions for scenery changes or intermissions between acts. The act divisions were probably the work of the editors of the Folio, while the standard scene divisions were added by 18th-century editors. Thus neither act nor scene divisions are integral parts of the play; and while I have tried to retain them as much as possible for ease of reference, I have not hesitated to remove certain scene divisions where they break up a continuous action and interfere with perception of the play's dramatic values. Scenes 3 and 4 of Act II, Scene 3 of Act IV, and Scenes 3 and 4 of Act V are incorporated in the immediately preceding scenes.

1SD Antony . . . Calpurnia Proper names are always something of a problem in Shakespeare for his spelling is Elizabethan and usually inconsistent. *Antony* is his spelling here, though correctly it should be *Antonius*, but a few lines later it becomes *Antonio* and I have not regularized because rhythm is involved. Shakespeare's spelling *Calphurnia*, however, has been changed to the more normal spelling of *Calpurnia* for the sake of clarity.

1 Calpurnia . . . Calpurnia These first three speeches are traditionally counted as one line of blank verse though no actors could possibly make them sound like a regular five-beat line. Shakespeare did not, in fact, write his plays *all* in blank verse, but convention has dictated that these and similar lines be handled in this way, and to avoid confusion in cross references I have been forced to follow the fashion, except in cases where the short, broken lines clearly contribute to the dramatic effect of the passage, e.g. crowd scenes and arguments.

113 **Caesar . . . sink** Caesar is traditionally described as a man, whatever his other faults, of great courage, and his extraordinary swimming ability is mentioned by both Plutarch and Suetonius. Cassius' attack on Caesar on these grounds thus tells us more about Cassius than Caesar.

114 **Aeneas, our great ancestor** Cassius refers here to the myth that Rome was founded by Aeneas after he escaped from Troy, carrying his father, Anchises, when the Greeks burned the city. See Vergil's *Aeneid*, Bk. II.

204–5 **He . . . music** According to Plutarch Antony was a riotous liver much given to luxury. Shakespeare makes more use of this tradition in his later play *Antony and Cleopatra* than here.

214 **deaf** This detail is Shakespeare's invention, and he uses it to suggest the human weakness which contrasts with Caesar's belief in his own godlike nature. The *falling-sickness*, i.e. epilepsy, referred to in l. 257 was, however, an infirmity to which the historical Julius Caesar was subject.

Act I, Scene 3

126 **Pompey's porch** The portico of the stone theater built by Pompey the Great in 55 B.C. In Plutarch, though not in Shakespeare, this theater is the scene of Caesar's assassination.

143 **praetor's chair** The formal seat of office of the praetor, a Roman magistrate or judge. Brutus at this time was one of the praetors.

Act II, Scene 1

29 **color** In this passage Brutus is musing, and his expression is therefore more elliptic and his thoughts more fragmentary than in his public discourse. Roughly, the passage means, 'Since Caesar now appears humble and mild we cannot pretend that we kill him because he is a tyrant, and therefore we must argue that power would corrupt him and we kill to forestall the abuses which are bound to come.'

40 **first of March** This is the Folio reading, but editors usually change to *ides of March* on the theory that since it is the ides of

March it would be foolish for Brutus to be so imprecise. See Appendix A for a full discussion of this line.

59 fifteen Most editors emend to *fourteen* because in l. 40 Brutus refers to *tomorrow* being the *first of March*, suggesting that it is before midnight, though he seems to regard daybreak as being the start of the new day, and day does not come until l. 103 or perhaps later. Shakespeare is never very realistic in his handling of actual time, however, and always manipulates it to suit his dramatic purposes. In l. 40 we have Brutus on the eve of the day of decision, pondering and concerned for the future, but by l. 103 the moment of crisis approaches and we are made aware of it by Lucius' announcement that it is already the ides of March. A similar dramatic adjustment of time also appears in ll. 61–2 where Brutus suggests that a number of sleepless nights have passed since he and Cassius talked. But in terms of the play itself we feel that events have rushed forward swiftly and that this night follows immediately the daylight conversations of Act I. Such use of 'double time' is standard in Shakespeare's plays.

66–9 The genius . . . insurrection The comparison in these lines is based upon a common Elizabethan understanding of the relation of man to the world, the microcosm to the macrocosm. According to Elizabethan theory the cosmos and all that it contained was made up of a series of corresponding parts, each identical in its structural arrangements and its dynamics to all the other parts. Thus, to concentrate on the area Brutus refers to, individual man resembles the state or *kingdom*, in that he too has a rightful king, the *genius*, and a populace, the *mortal instruments*. Revolution, *insurrection*, occurs when the baser fears and appetites rebel against their rightful ruler, the reason or genius. Shakespeare makes regular use of this microcosm-macrocosm theory, and it appears again in *Julius Caesar* in I.3 where the disorders in the political realm, i.e. the plans to kill Caesar, are reflected in the cosmos, e.g. the shooting stars, and in the realm of nature. For a full discussion of this theory see E. M. W. Tillyard, *The Elizabethan World Picture* (London, 1943).

107

120 **high-sighted** This particular phrase well illustrates the peculiar difficulty of glossing a Shakespearian play and saying *exactly* what a given word or phrase means. Here the general sense is one of an aspiring tyrant, Caesar, who is both rising upwards and has a keen and penetrating eye for discovering his enemies. More particularly, *high-sighted* may refer to (1) haughtiness, the eyes elevated upwards, (2) a hunting falcon whose high position allows it to watch the land below for prey, (3) a high-aiming desire for utmost political power. All three interpretations are equally possible—all have been proposed by previous editors —and rather than choose one over the others it seems best to accept the fact that all three meanings are compressed, in the manner typical of poetry but not of discursive prose, into this single phrase. Since the word *range* here is a technical term from falconry, it seems possible however that the primary reference is to a hunting falcon; and Shakespeare frequently draws his imagery from this sport.

193SD **Clock strikes** Editors have delighted to point out that since clocks were not invented until the 13th century, Shakespeare is guilty of an anachronism here. He has worse 'blunders' elsewhere in the play, for his Romans climb to the chimney tops of Elizabethan London (I.1.41), wear *hats* 'pluck'd about their ears' (II.1.173), and dress in doublets (I.2.268). To condemn Shakespeare for these anachronisms is to judge him by the laws of history, not of literature. *Julius Caesar* is not a historical study of Rome, nor is it a picture of London in 1599; rather it is an image compounded of Rome in the last days of the Republic and London at the end of the Tudor reign, and what it images is neither of these but the perpetual situation of political man attempting to find a workable way of governing the world and himself. Somewhat paradoxically the anachronisms contribute to rather than detract from the effect of the play, for they advertise the fact that the meaning is universal rather than local, that it applies to all men and not just those of 1st-century Rome.

302 **wound** Plutarch tells how Portia to prove her bravery cut herself with a razor and bled until she fainted.

Act II, Scene 2

46 We are As printed in the Folio this line reads 'We heare two lyons, litter'd in one day.' Since this does not make sense, all editors emend to *We are*. It may be that the Folio *heare* is a misprint of 'we(a)re.'

89 tinctures . . . cognizance This sequence is difficult because it contains several elements not strictly parallel. *Tincture* and *cognizance* are both heraldic terms—though *tincture* also means 'elixir' or 'essential spirit'—referring to colors and emblems in a coat-of-arms. *Stains* and *relics* both suggest holy properties of a martyr, i.e. a handkerchief dipped in his blood. The general sense of the line is, of course, that Caesar will dignify and honor the Roman people, but it should be noted that Decius maintains here the ambiguous manner of speaking he employs throughout this speech. Caesar thinks he means that the living Caesar will so honor Rome, but Decius really means that the murdering of Caesar will revivify Rome and distinguish those who have killed him.

129SD Enter Artemidorus At this point, and again after l. 144, editors usually put in scene divisions, and the last 59 lines of Act II thus become Scenes 3 and 4. I have, however, omitted these two short scene divisions in order not to interfere with the rapid progression of events moving toward a climax.

Act III, Scene 1

50–1 Caesar . . . satisfied Ben Jonson in his *Discoveries*, printed 1641, quotes an alternate version of these lines, 'Caesar did never wrong but with just cause.' Jonson found the idea illogical and ridiculous—though it is not when one considers that it is not Shakespeare's thought but the dramatic character, Caesar's—and he mocks it again in his play, *The Staple of News* (1626), where the Prologue says, 'Cry you mercy, *you never did wrong, but with just cause.*' Some critics have concluded that this is the way the line originally read, and that the version in the Folio, and printed in this text, is a revision, perhaps by Shakespeare, made in response to general criticism of the original.

Such speculation is interesting, but it provides no secure basis for an emendation of the lines as we have them.

Act III, Scene 2

197–8 Pompey's . . . blood Plutarch mentions that during Caesar's assassination Pompey's statue ran blood. This would relate to the Elizabethan belief that a corpse's wounds flowed again in the presence of its murderer, for while Caesar had not killed Pompey with his own hand, he had indirectly brought about his death in the civil wars preceding the events of the play.

206 Here is himself According to Plutarch Antony did not actually show the mob the body of Caesar, but Shakespeare heightens the dramatic impact of the scene by allowing Antony to use the body as the culmination of his successful attempt to sway the crowd.

Act IV, Scene 1

38 On . . . imitations This line has been much emended by various editors to improve its sense, but taken as a whole the meaning of the passage is clear. Antony is accusing Lepidus of lacking originality of thought and points out that this quality is apparent in his taste, for he prefers those things, *objects*, works of art, *arts*, and second-hand ideas and things, *imitations*, which have already been praised by other men and then discarded.

49–50 stake . . . enemies The metaphor here derives from the popular Elizabethan sport of bearbaiting. The bear was tied to a stake in the center of an arena, and dogs were set on him. The fight was vicious and to the finish, a spectacle of the utmost savagery.

Act IV, Scene 2

1SD Enter Brutus The scene has now shifted to the camp of Brutus at Sardis in Greece.

53SD Manent Brutus and Cassius At this point, working on the theory that the scene changes from the plain where Brutus and Cassius meet to the inside of Brutus' tent, the majority of editors mark a new scene, Scene 3. But the situation here provides a striking instance of how the Elizabethan stage worked. At one moment Brutus and Cassius are standing on the plain giving orders, and the next moment, without changing place, they are inside Brutus' tent arguing. The only visible change has been the exit of their officers. To mark a change of scene here would suggest a delay and rearrangement of the stage, and we would lose the continuity of playing which was a regular feature of the bare Elizabethan stage, though not of ours; and in this particular case the building, impetuous anger of Cassius would be blocked and the power of the scene lost.

76 supporting robbers Brutus' charge here is that Caesar was involved in corrupt practices and allowed his political favorites a certain amount of graft. This is the first time Brutus has made this particular charge, and earlier he has stressed the fact that Caesar had not yet engaged in any dishonest activities but might become corrupt if allowed to gain great power. Shakespeare was at this point in the play following Plutarch very closely and picked up this detail from his source.

78–9 And sell . . .' grasped thus As Brutus speaks the line 'trash as may be grasped thus,' he closes his hand as if to enfold money, and the confined area of his closed fist is thus contrasted to 'the mighty space' and wide freedom provided by their honor.

102 spleen Throughout this description of Cassius' anger, Brutus has reference to the Elizabethan—and Aristotelean— humor theory of character. According to this theory there were four radical 'humors' or character types: the saturnine, the melancholic, the choleric, and the sanguine. Each of these humors was thought to derive from an excess of one of the basic fluids of the body—in the case of the choleric or passionate man, such as Brutus pictures Cassius, the fluid was bile, and it derived from the spleen. This is the *venom* which Brutus says Cassius must swallow rather than venting in anger.

189SD Enter a Poet According to Plutarch this 'poet' was the cynic philosopher Marcus Phaonius who upon entering quoted Nestor's line from Homer's *Iliad*. 'But listen to me. You are both younger than I.'

253 ff. Had you your letters . . . At this point begins the so-called 'duplicate revelation of Portia's death.' We know al-

111

ready from Brutus' preceding discussion with Cassius that he is fully aware of Portia's death, but now he pretends to Messala that he is unaware of the event. Most modern editors have argued that Shakespeare first wrote the present scene, ll. 253 ff., and then deciding that these lines failed to suggest Brutus' real love for Portia, the playwright went back and wrote the scene with Cassius ll. 210 ff., in which Brutus reveals that he is deeply touched. But somehow, the argument goes, the scene with Messala was not cut from the manuscript used in printing the play, and as a result we have both scenes, and Brutus is placed in the position of a man who has contrived a scene in which he can display his vaunted 'philosophy.' All of this is the airiest speculation based on a theory that Brutus is such an honest man that he could not be guilty of this shamming. Against this theory I would simply point out two facts: (1) that there is nothing at all suspicious about the text at this point; it is perfectly clear and consistent and gives not the slightest evidence of any awkward insertions or corruptions; (2) that we are not free to delete actions and events from any play because we believe they are inconsistent with the picture of the character we have built up in our minds from previous events, for we do not have a complete view of any character until we have seen *all* that he does in a play, down to his very last line.

351 **leaden mace** Sleep is compared here to an arresting officer who in Elizabethan times signaled the act of arrest by laying the mace, his staff of office, on the shoulder of his victim.

Act V, Scene 1

80 **held Epicurus strong** believed strongly in Epicurus' theory. Epicurus, a Greek philosopher, born 342 B.C., argued that omens are to be disregarded because the gods do not interfere in the affairs of men. That is, they neither warn men of the future through omens, nor do they predestine the course of events.

Act V, Scene 2

6SD **Alarums** Another scene, Scene 3, is usually begun here, but it is clear from the beginning of the actual battle with Scene 2 that what we have is a continuous movement of flow and ebb in the fight. The technique is very much like that of the films where the camera moves rapidly from one part of the battlefield to another and manages while using only a few actors to convey the sense of a gigantic struggle involving rapid movement and quick changes of fortune. The scene, 4, which is usually marked at 2.118 of this edition, is also left out.

112 Tharsus An alternative spelling of Tarsus. According to Plutarch the body was sent to Thasos, an island off the coast of Thrace; and it may be that Tharsus represents a misreading on the part of either Shakespeare or the printer.

117 three a clock In lines 67 ff. above we are told that the sun is setting. Shakespeare is here, as elsewhere in the play, simply manipulating time for his own dramatic purposes. He wanted the comparison of the dying Cassius to the setting sun earlier, and now he wants to continue the battle scene. Historically, of course, the second battle took place twenty days after the first.

125 [Brutus.] The Folio provides no speech ascription here, and some recent editors have conjectured that Brutus was too well known to need to announce his name. They have therefore assigned this line to Lucilius who shortly afterwards pretends to be Brutus. But, it seems to me, Brutus is not merely announcing his name here; rather he is following Cato's lead and rallying his followers by showing them that their leader is still on the field.

Act V, Scene 3

76 elements Literally, Antony is referring to the belief that man, like the rest of nature, is compounded of the various elements—earth, air, fire, and water—and as a result of this is also a mixture of the various humors. But Shakespeare's metaphors always do more than provide instances of contemporary medical and other beliefs. Here, Antony is summing up Brutus' life and announcing what the play has shown: that Brutus, like other men, is a curious mixed creature, made up of incongruous elements, body and soul, matter and mind. The central irony of the play is, of course, that Brutus, who now lies here a dead body, has maintained always that he was all mind, spirit, rationality.

113

APPENDIX A

Text and Date

The Tragedy of Julius Caesar was first printed in the Folio edition of Shakespeare's complete works brought out in 1623, six years after his death in 1616. The play was, however, written and staged by 1599. Our evidence for this date consists of a description by Thomas Platter, a Swiss traveler, of a performance of the play in that year: 'After lunch on September 21st, at about two o'clock, I and my party crossed the river, and there in the house with the thatched roof we saw an excellent performance of the tragedy of the first Emperor Julius Caesar with about fifteen characters; after the play, according to their custom they did a most elegant and curious dance, two dressed in men's clothes, and two in women's.' The 'house with the thatched roof' was probably the Globe Theater, built on the Bankside in 1599 by Shakespeare's company, then the Lord Chamberlain's Men; and the 'elegant and curious dance' was the jig with which it was common practice to conclude performances.

The Folio text is our only authentic text of *Julius Caesar,* and as the texts of Shakespeare's plays go, it is remarkably free of corruptions and printing errors. Modern bibliographical opinion is fairly well agreed that in this case the compositor setting up type for the First Folio was probably working from a clean copy of some kind, perhaps the theatrical promptbook. The unusually full number of stage directions suggests a manuscript connected in some way with the actual production of the play.

But despite the cleanness of the text of *Caesar,* an editor of the play is still faced with a number of decisions about what to print and how to print it, and I should like to offer a brief explanation of the general practices of this edition, practices

114

which in some instances result in a somewhat different version of the text than is usual in older, and even in some newer, editions.

The most general rule has been to follow the Folio whenever it makes sense—even a somewhat awkward sense—rather than substitute for the Folio reading an emendation of some sort which seems to make better sense of a particular kind. Thus at II.1.40 where Brutus asks Lucius, his servant, 'Is not tomorrow, boy, the first of March?' most editors from the 18th century on have changed the line to read, 'Is not tomorrow . . . the ides of March?' Their reasoning has been that since in the play tomorrow *is* the 15th of March and the day Caesar is assassinated, then Shakespeare must have written *ides,* and this word must have been misread by the copyist or the printer as *first.* I do not share these editors' faith in Shakespeare's strict accuracy in handling time—this particular play is filled with instances of the chronology being manipulated for dramatic effect (e.g. V.2.67ff.). Furthermore, it is possible to see, I believe, that failure to know the date is characteristic of the impractical Brutus, who is apt to forget where he placed his book and overlooks more important, practical matters, such as the need to kill Antony and the strategy which dictates that you allow the enemy to come to you rather than leave a favorable position and seek him out. Whether you accept my particular explanation or not, the fact remains that the Folio reading is clearly *first of March,* and since some kind of sense can be made of this, it seems better to print what the Folio gives us. I have done the same in a number of other places where changes have traditionally been made by the editors, and have explained in the Notes the reason in each case for restoring the original reading.

There are, of course, a few places where the Folio reading is almost surely wrong; see, for example, III.I.43, where the original reads *lane of children,* and where all editors emend to *law of children.* But these obvious errors are few in *Julius Caesar,* and by far the greatest number of emendations and changes in the text have resulted not from editors' attempts

115

to make sense out of confusion but from their desire to pres
on the play at hand their own interpretations of character an
their own view of what a play is. This is certainly the case i
the rejection by many editors of the second revelation o
Portia's death, IV.3.253ff., where the *only* grounds for castin
doubt on the passage is a theory that Brutus is far too fine
man to pretend that he hasn't heard about his wife's deat
when he actually has. The majority of editorial emendations
however, have come about not from any theory of characte
but rather from a 'realistic' view of the nature of drama
Thus we are told in the first scene of the play that it is mor
realistic at line 16 for Marullus to continue questioning th
Cobbler than for Flavius to break in. And when Lucius, on th
night before the assassination, returns to Brutus, II.1.59, an
tells him that 'March is wasted fifteen days,' the majority o
editors emend to *fourteen days,* on the realistic grounds tha
the sun has not yet risen and that the Roman day did no
begin until sunrise. In these and other cases I have returne
to the Folio reading in the belief that a play is not written t
mirror literal reality, or whatever we take to be reality, bu
is an imaginative construct in which the author manipulate
literal reality to suit his dramatic purposes.

Realism has also had its effect on punctuation and stag
directions. In I.2, after Casca has told Brutus and Cassiu
that Caesar fell down and foamed at the mouth when th
crown was offered him, Brutus remarks, according to the Folio
' 'Tis very like he hath the Falling sicknesse.' Which means, 1
take it, that Brutus is saying, 'It sounds as if Caesar ha
epilepsy.' But practically every editor has inserted some mar
of punctuation between *like* and *he* which makes the line mean
'It is probable that he did so, *for* he has epilepsy.' The reaso
offered for this change is the realistic one that Brutus ha
known Caesar for a long time and would certainly have know
that he had epilepsy. To which I might reply, arguing o
equally realistic grounds, that Caesar's epilepsy was a care
fully guarded secret. But the argument cannot be settled o
realistic grounds, and since the original reading of the lin

116

makes good sense—though I can see no particular dramatic value in it—I have printed it as it stands in the Folio. But in most places it is impossible to retain the original punctuation in a text designed for a modern reader, since the Elizabethans did not punctuate as we do. Every editor must devise some method of punctuating which will give the logical sense of the passage without destroying its dramatic flow. The task is made all the more difficult by the fact that Shakespeare frequently plays fast and loose with grammar, so that while his meaning is usually, though not always, clear, it is impossible to point his paragraphs according to the rules of English grammar. Every editor I am sure sighs with relief when he sees a period finally arriving in one of Shakespeare's long paragraphs where phrase is built on phrase and clause separated from clause by digressive elements. Suffice it to say that the punctuation of the present edition is offered, without pride, as one more attempt to reconcile the contrary demands of logic on the one hand and dramatic movement on the other. My one consistent practice has been to reduce the number of exclamation marks with which this and other Shakespearian texts are usually sprinkled. My theory here has been that it was possible in Shakespeare's time and is in our own for an actor to deliver a line forcefully and emphatically without shouting it.

Stage directions, as I have noted, are in this play remarkably full, though it is noticeable that entrances are more carefully marked than exits, probably for the reason that in the theater it is getting an actor on stage in time which counts—he can be trusted to get off by himself. Following the lines laid down by the general editors of the Yale Shakespeare, I have not, however, marked these missing exits, nor have I indicated certain actions on the part of the characters which are clearly called for by the lines. The reader will have no difficulty in supplying these stage directions for himself. Settings of scenes are not supplied since they do not appear in the Folio, and the lines usually inform us where we are very quickly. I have been hesitant to add the names of characters to groups entering and exiting when the Folio does not have them.

117

Act divisions are marked in the Folio, but scene divisions are not, and I have in most instances followed standard practice in designating scenes. In some places, however, where marking the end of one scene and the beginning of another obviously would break the flow of the action or destroy the quality of the dramatic movement at that point, I have refrained from starting new scenes. Such situations occur at the end of Act II, in the middle of Act IV, and in the middle of Act V. My reasons for leaving out the usual scene designations at these points are fully explained at the appropriate point in the notes which follow the text. As a result of this practice scene numbers and line numbers of this edition will not always be identical with those of other editions.

Line numbering in this edition is also affected by my approach to the half lines which occur in the Folio versions of this and other Shakespearian plays. For example, at V.2.66 Titinius and Messala discover the body of Cassius on the ground, and the Folio prints their lines in this manner:

> *Messala.* Is not that hee?
> *Titinius.* No, this was he *Messala.*

Put these two lines together and you get a fairly regular line of blank verse, though there are eleven syllables in this particular case if you pronounce each syllable of *Messala.* There are a great many such lines in *Caesar,* and the usual practice beginning with the 18th-century editors has been to print these half lines as a single line by echeloning them in this manner:

> *Messala.* Is not that he?
> *Titinius.*   No, this was he, Messala.

Though it is difficult to imagine how two actors would manage to make these lines sound like a single line of blank verse, still there seems no reason not to print this particular line in the conventional manner. Here the characters are responding to one another and speaking in close sympathy, so the visual effect of union achieved by printing their lines as part of one unit seems fitting. But in the many instances where characters

118

are quarreling and each half line is a counterblow to its predecessor, where evenness and harmony are lost, then it seems a misrepresentation of the quality of the scene to print the lines in a way which suggests continuation and flow. For example in the quarrel scene between Brutus and Cassius in IV.2.104ff. the Folio prints three of the lines in this manner:

> *Brutus.* Ile use you for my Mirth, yea for my Laughter
> When you are Waspish.
> *Cassius.* Is it come to this?

Which in many modern editions is printed thus:

> *Brutus.* I'll use you for my mirth, yea, for my laughter,
> When you are waspish.
> *Cassius.*   Is it come to this?

The Folio printing seems to catch far better the quarrelsome mood of the exchange. Of course if every line in the play somehow worked out regularly then an editor would have no choice except to try to rediscover the original lineation destroyed in the Folio printing. But there are many lines in the play which are clearly most irregular, e.g., IV.2.86–93, and it seems clear that Shakespeare wrote *plays* in which he suited his meters to his dramatic purpose, not long dramatic poems in which he worked within an invariable metrical scheme. For this reason I have felt free to print the half lines in a way that seemed to me to agree with the tonal quality of the scene of which they are a part, rather than count syllables and mechanically scan to see if when put together any two short lines resemble in some way one line of blank verse.

APPENDIX B

Sources

Vergil's *Georgics,* Appian's *History, The Mirror for Magistrates,* and an academic play, *Caesar's Revenge,* produced by students at Oxford, all perhaps contributed something to Shakespeare's *Julius Caesar.* But Shakespeare's principal source was Plutarch's *Lives* as translated by Sir Thomas North and printed in 1579, and again in 1595, under the title, *The Lives of the Noble Grecians and Romanes.* North did not actually work from the original Greek of Plutarch but from a French translation of Jaques Amyot printed in 1559. The reader who is interested in a full discussion of all the sources which have been proposed for *Julius Caesar* may consult Kenneth Muir, *Shakespeare's Sources, Comedies and Tragedies* (London, 1957), 1, 187–200. The sections of North's Plutarch used by Shakespeare in writing his Roman plays are readily available in *Shakespeare's Plutarch,* ed. W. W. Skeat, London, 1875.

The details of *Julius Caesar* are often Shakespeare's inventions, e.g. the language of the crowd, or the exchanges between Brutus and his servant Lucius. But the main events of the play are invariably derived from North's Plutarch. In certain rare instances Shakespeare adhered very closely to the wording of the original. Here, for example, is North's version of Portia's impassioned plea to be admitted to Brutus' confidence:

> I being, O *Brutus* (sayed she) the daughter of *Cato,* was maried unto thee, not to be thy bedfellowe and companion in bedde and at borde onelie, like a harlot: but to be partaker also with thee, of thy good and evill fortune. Nowe for thy selfe, I can finde no cause of faulte in thee touchinge our matche: but for my parte, howe may I showe my duetie towardes thee, & howe muche I woulde

doe for thy sake, if I can not constantlie beare a secret
mischaunce or griefe with thee, which requireth secrecy
& fidelity? I confesse, that a womans wit commonly is too
weake to keepe a secret safely: but yet, *Brutus,* good
educacion, and the companie of vertuous men, have some
power to reforme the defect of nature. And for my selfe,
I have this benefit moreover: that I am the daughter of
Cato, and wife of *Brutus.* This notwithstanding, I did not
trust to any of these things before: untill that now I have
found by experience, that no paine nor griefe whatsoever
can overcome me. With these wordes she shewed him
herselfe.

Compare to this Portia's lines in II.1.281–304.

But in the majority of cases Shakespeare merely took the
bare outlines of his scene from North, and then proceeded to
elaborate, to put flesh on the bare bones of event. As an example of this practice we may take the most famous speech
in the play, Antony's oration in the market place over the body
of Caesar. In Plutarch, Caesar's will is made known to the
populace by some unspecified means before Antony's funeral
oration, and the people are already inflamed when Antony
makes the speech described by Plutarch, according to North,
in the following way:

Afterwards, when *Caesars* body was brought into the
market place, *Antonius* making his funerall oration in
praise of the dead, according to the aunciant custom of
Rome, & perceiving that his wordes moved the common
people to compassion: he framed his eloquence to make
their harts yerne the more, and taking *Caesars* gowne all
bloudy in his hand, he layed it open to the sight of them
all, shewing what a number of cuts and holes it had upon
it. Therewithall the people fell presently into such a rage
and mutinie, that there was no more order kept amongst
the common people. For some of them cryed out, kill the
murtherers: others plucked up formes, tables, and stalles
about the market place, as they had done before at the

121

> funeralls of *Clodius*, and having layed them all on a heape
> together, they set them on fire, and thereupon did put the
> bodye of *Caesar*, and burnt it in the middest of the most
> holy places.

Shakespeare also had from Plutarch a brief description of
Antony's oratorical style: 'He used a manner of phrase in his
speeche, called Asiatik, which caried the best grace and
estimation at that time, and was much like to his manners and
life: for it was full of ostentation, foolishe braverie, and vaine
ambition.' From these scanty materials Shakespeare fashioned
the magnificent funeral oration beginning 'Friends, Romans,
countrymen,' and this kind of elaboration is typical of his
methods throughout most of the play.

In writing *Julius Caesar* Shakespeare drew on three of
Plutarch's *Lives*, those of Brutus, Julius Caesar, and Antony.
Taken together these three lives contain a vast amount of
material, of which Shakespeare used only a fraction, and something must be said of Shakespeare's principles of selection,
i.e. why did he choose this detail and leave that out? By ap-
proaching the source in this way we can perhaps gain some
insight into Shakespeare's artistic purpose in *Julius Caesar*.

The major elements of the plot were dictated to the playwright by historical fact as recorded by Plutarch. The play
had to include the conspiracy, the assassination, the speeches
to the crowd, and the defeat and death of Brutus and Cassius
with the assumption of power by the Triumvirate. These events
define the major arc of the action; they are 'what happens' in
the most literal sense; and around them Shakespeare shaped
his play. But most writers, and Shakespeare particularly, are
always concerned not with merely telling a story but with ex-
ploring the nature of what happens and explaining how it
happens. Presumably then, the particular scenes and events
which Shakespeare chose from Plutarch and included in his
play are those which to his mind constituted the clearest explanation of the nature and causes of the major historical
events; and, similarly, his additions to and elaboration of

122

Plutarch's material were also directed toward explanation of these main events.

In general, Shakespeare seems to have borrowed from Plutarch scenes and events which fall roughly into two categories. The first category has as its major theme the irrational, while the second has the antithetical theme of the rational. That is, Shakespeare selected unerringly from Plutarch two kinds of scenes: those in which the dark, the supernatural, the unexplained, the emotional, the primitive forces in the world, in history, and in man are stressed; and those in which the clear, the rational, the logical, the planned, and the controlled elements are stressed.

As examples of the first kind of scene we might note the enormous amounts of the supernatural which appear in the play: auguries, foreknowledge of the future, the feast of the Lupercal, the portents of Caesar's death, the appearance of his ghost, the ominous dreams. Or on the social and historical level we have the irrational and ignorant crowd, never constant but moving always in response to its feelings of the moment and its greed; and the nervous inability of the conspirators to agree even on such a simple matter as where the sun rises. On the personal level the play includes an enormous number of events showing man's inability to control himself by the light of reason, events which range from Lucius' inability to keep awake and Brutus' forgetfulness about where he placed his book to Portia's nervous fear about what is going on in the Senate—so excited is she that she forgets to tell the messenger his message—and Cinna the poet's compulsive wandering forth to his death at the hands of the crowd, though his conscious mind recognizes the danger.

At the same time that Shakespeare was lifting these events from Plutarch's narrative and weaving them into his play, he was also selecting and enlarging on scenes in which men display themselves as rational, constant, clear-thinking individuals enunciating ideal principles and capable of making plans to achieve desired ends. Using reasoned political arguments, at least in part, Cassius persuades Brutus to join the

123

conspiracy, and Brutus persuades himself on the rational grounds that Caesar must be prevented before he becomes a danger to the Roman state. Caesar stresses his freedom from normal human fear for self in going to the Senate against Calpurnia's pleadings, and once there he neglects to read the warning handed him by Artemidorus and announces his eternal constancy in the matter of the banishment of Publius Cimber. Portia proves the freedom of her mind from her body by cutting herself with a razor. Putting his trust in man's reasonable nature, Brutus addresses the mob in cold, logical terms, and in the name of such ideals as reason and justice he kills Caesar, refuses to kill Antony, and forces the battle at Philippi.

Although Shakespeare does not in Julius Caesar keep the two threads separate, in selecting his material from Plutarch he culled out events which, within the limitations of length imposed by dramatic form, could be used to set up an antithesis on several levels between the planned and the unplanned, the logical and the illogical, the reason and the passions, the dark and the light. This conflict runs through the play, and each of the major historical events which constitute the main action is both an example of this conflict and a result of the working of these opposed forces.

APPENDIX C

Reading List

KENNETH BURKE, "Antony in Behalf of the Play," in *The Philosophy of Literary Form,* Baton Rouge, 1941.

HARLEY GRANVILLE-BARKER, *Prefaces to Shakespeare,* 1st Series, London, 1927.

G. WILSON KNIGHT, *The Imperial Theme,* London, 1931, chs. 2, 3.

HELGE KÖKERITZ, *Shakespeare's Pronunciation,* New Haven, 1953.

—— *Shakespeare's Names. A Pronouncing Dictionary,* New Haven, 1959.

M. W. MAC CALLUM, *Shakespeare's Roman Plays and Their Background,* London, 1910.

JOHN PALMER, *Political Characters of Shakespeare,* London, 1945.

BRENTS STIRLING, *Unity in Shakespearian Tragedy: The Interplay of Theme and Character,* New York, 1956. The relevant chapter, "Or Else Were This a Savage Spectacle," is reprinted in *Shakespeare: Modern Essays in Criticism,* ed. Leonard Dean, New York, 1957.

HAROLD S. WILSON, *On the Design of Shakespearian Tragedy,* Toronto, 1957.

125